I0532394

SHELLEY E. MOORE

THROUGH
A
BLUE-EYED
LENS

A MEMPHIS MEMOIR

This book is dedicated to my sons and their families.

Eli, Larisa and Luna

Joshua, Laura, Viva and Wolf

I love you all.

Larisa, Luna, Eli, Viva, Josh, Wolf, Laura
New Jersey beach, 2019

"The story of a young woman attending Memphis City Schools in the years surrounding Dr. King's assassination, *Through A Blue-Eyed Lens* poignantly reaffirms Faulkner's truth that the past is never dead nor really even the past. Anyone interested in Memphis social and racial history should read this book, because what played out for Shelley more than fifty years ago is still playing out for us all today."

Daniel B. Hatzenbuehler, *Long-time Memphian and Rhodes College Trustee*

"Shelley takes us on a poignant journey from another time. Her story is filled with heartbreak, bitter truths and redemption."

Willy Bearden, *Television, radio and film, Memphis, TN*

"Ms. Moore's Memphis memoir, *Through A Blue-Eyed Lens*, offers the reader a powerful narrative of her personal experiences in the 1960s, set against the backdrop of public school desegregation, the civil rights movement and the assassination of Dr. King."

Mike Cody, *Memphis Attorney and Civil Rights Advocate*

"I found this humble story to be a page-turner. Born the same year as Shelley but far from the civil rights action of the 1960s, the story of her adolescence in Memphis brought home to me the gravity of the struggle. This is a valuable book, especially for anyone who grew up in a non-diverse community far from the American South."

Deborah Paulson, *Retired Professor, University of Wyoming*

CONTENTS

Shelley, 1955

REMEMBERING

Benjamin Lawson Hooks was born in Memphis in 1925, grandson of the second Black woman to graduate from an American college. Raised with a deep respect for education, Ben set his sights on becoming an attorney. When, as a Black student, he was refused admittance to law schools in the State of Tennessee, Ben went north to DePaul University School of Law to earn his degree. He then returned to Memphis to establish his practice. Ben's legacy grew to include positions as civil rights leader, pastor of two churches simultaneously (one in Memphis, the other in Detroit), Criminal Court Judge, FCC Commissioner and Executive Director of the NAACP.

Ben's wife, Frances Dancy Hooks, also a Memphis native, was a powerhouse in her own right. A take-charge woman who wore many hats, she was Ben's stalwart companion, partner, supporter and advisor for nearly fifty years, until her husband's death in 2010. In her position as guidance counselor at Carver High School, she proved to be a tremendous force in the lives of thousands of young people who benefitted from her sage encouragement and tutelage. Frances died in 2016.

Frances and Ben were instrumental in founding The National Civil Rights Museum in Memphis, which opened to the public in 1991. Located at the site of the Lorraine Motel where Martin Luther King, Jr. was killed in 1968, the museum remains a profoundly important national archive and interactive education center that is visited annually by tens of thousands of world citizens.

Just a young, green shoot of a girl, I was incredibly fortunate to know and be influenced by Ben and Frances Hooks, to hang out in the shadows of two courageous and tireless pioneers who dedicated their lives to civil rights and social justice. The City of Memphis saw fit to name its contemporary main branch on Poplar Avenue the Benjamin L. Hooks Public Library. Frances is clearly honored in that naming as well.

I have written *Through A Blue-Eyed Lens* in this library, always seated at the same table. Each time I pass through the building's lobby, I'm drawn to the inspiring photo collage of the couple that greets and informs all who enter.

The Benjamin L. Hooks Library

AUTHOR'S NOTES

Music has always provided important theater to life. No matter the genre, it tends to walk right in and take up residence in the nooks and crannies of memory banks, causing reflexive responses to songs and compositions. Associated with people and events in our lives, opening riffs and familiar refrains can bring smiles to our faces or tears to our eyes. Because songs and artists from the sixties and seventies reflect so many collective experiences, I referenced that music in my headings. Hopefully, some of my choices strike a chord or awaken a memory for you. Composer credits can be found in the Index.

I considered using terms of the day throughout my text to best authentically and accurately reflect the tone of the nineteen sixties:

"Colored"... "Negro"... and "n****r"

Except for a few specific quotes, I simply couldn't talk myself into it, knowing that doing so would serve no effective purpose.

In recognition and support of the Black Lives Matter movement, I've chosen to follow the lead of *The New York Times* in capitalizing the word "Black" when the descriptor refers to people. I agree with their reasoning behind not capitalizing "brown" and "white" in the same context. If not already familiar with it, I strongly encourage a read of the following editorial:

Why We're Capitalizing Black - The New York Times

July 5, 2020

I have included recollections of several former classmates and family members who have generously lent their voices to this endeavor. The words are their own. Grateful for the compelling stories, I am taken by the range of experience and emotion expressed in their pieces. Some of them clearly have books of their own to write.

And finally, my text includes several letters that *figuratively* represent actual interactions or conversations that took place during the decade of 1962-1972. In monologue form, I have used my adult voice, vocabulary and perspective in reconstructing these memories. I hope that they help to animate the tension of some relationships and the intimacy of others.

PREFACE

I Could Write A Book

Everyone has a story to tell but even as I write this book, I'm not totally convinced that my reflections and long-germinating narrative need be added to the autobiographies and memoirs lining the shelves of bookstores and libraries – all of which are under threat of becoming extinct repositories of hard copy. That said, here goes. At sixty-six and counting, my body and mind are less reliable with each passing year. Crisp details have become muddled. I've forgotten far more about my youth than I remember, so it's time to capture what I can from my personal storehouse, if only in the form of a figurative snapshot or pinhole.

Collective memories have also shifted and paled over the years. Some of us remember shared experiences differently or don't recall them at all. That fact has become abundantly and often humorously clear as I've compared recollections and timelines with family and friends.

From the moment I realized I could crawl, I've been unable to sit still for long. You who know me well can attest to that. I recently came across my kindergarten report card, which called me out for not focusing on the task at hand. Without much persistence, patience, or commitment to hard work, I used to demand, or at least expect, a fabulous result with minimal effort. I've clearly made some progress on that front, as one doesn't set out to put this many words onto paper without sitting still for reasonably long periods of time.

In writing this book, it would have been much safer and simpler for me to make claims backed up by data and dates. But statistics and numbers don't begin to explain what took place in Memphis during the decade that spanned 1962 to 1972. In bookending those years, I've tried to be transparent, even vulnerable, as I set loose bits of that history and transpose mere fact into substantive and emotional content. In an attempt to humor myself and hopefully amuse you, I've injected a bit of levity into a weighty story line by adding some lighter interludes.

This is not meant to be an epic saga of my life. Most of my missteps and accomplishments haven't found their way onto these pages. If you and your shared experiences with me aren't included in this book, you're not forgotten. These are simply flashes and fragments of a very specific time period in my early years. Any errors or critical omissions are mine alone. I'm writing from my singular perspective and recall; in no way do I attempt to speak for anyone else, Black or white, living or deceased. I mean no harm.

It's Been a Long Time Coming

It's entirely possible that I write this to myself as much as I write it for others, as the process of transcribing memories onto paper has been quite cathartic for me. The 1960s and 1970s witnessed a Memphis moment, an instance illustrated by unique relationships, interactions and events. I was there by a twist of fate, not by choice. My part in that chapter of history is but a microscopic blip, its only significance being the interconnectedness of people, place and time. Some will recognize themselves or others in these stories, people who through luck, common cause, serendipity or sheer coincidence crossed paths during that decade in Memphis, Tennessee.

I don't know how it feels to be anything other than a white woman. I grew up a privileged white girl in an extremely segregated and racist environment. I feel so very fortunate to have spent ten of my most formative years in Memphis, where I was confronted with choices about how to respond to that landscape. I was faced with options: about how to address people, how to refer to people, how to shape my world and who to include in that sphere. I ended up making different choices than most of my white peers. Not necessarily better. Different. Because of those decisions, I learned at an early age how it feels to cross lines, to challenge perceptions and assumptions, to make wildly unpopular decisions and to face unsettling and unpredictable consequences.

The nineteen-sixties saw scores of Memphians of every age and skin tone struggling against the demons of widespread and deep-seated racism. Those of us who were part of that struggle learned, benefitted from and relied on each other's love and support during very difficult years. Every single aspect and corner of our world, including where we lived, went to school, worked and recreated was touched, tainted and controlled by Jim Crow restrictions. Across the South, an unmistakable defining line separated the opportunities, the potentials and the rights of Black and white citizens.

Post World War II is often referred to as "the good old days," but *What a Wonderful World* didn't apply to many American families. The concept of a lovely home, tucked into a manicured landscape, set off by a picket fence, was realized by some but proved to be an impossible dream for many. That dream remained in perpetual suspension for families ensnared in racial discrimination and cyclical poverty. Those disparities and disappointments were not lost on many Memphians then and they aren't today in 2021, as one quarter of the city's residents live in poverty.

It would have been unthinkable for me to write about my experiences from that decade without weaving threads into the narrative of what was transpiring in our city, both socially and politically. Those were fluid, empowering and frightening times for Memphis and its people. Lives were turned upside down and inside out as change began to take hold.

The prevailing constructs of white supremacy and privilege, increasingly examined and dissected under the microscope of social justice and equality, were not holding up well under such scrutiny. Change was coming. Ready or not.

Fire and Rain

The primary focal points of this book are the years that witnessed, among many other noteworthy events, the desegregation of the Memphis City Schools and the assassination in that city of Dr. Martin Luther King, Jr. I've read many accounts by others, both Black and white, who were students during that time. If I had read those stories before beginning my own narrative, I could be accused of plagiarism and rightly so. The fact that many of us have used exactly the same wording, terminology and phraseology is no coincidence; it's a reflection of the fact that our experiences so closely mimicked and paralleled one another during those defining years in the American South.

There is no question that student bodies in other locales endured far more contentious junior and high school years than we did in Memphis. I'm grateful to have gained that perspective because, even though the desegregation of our schools was life-altering and not always pleasant for those of us involved, for the most part we weren't faced with the extreme vitriol and frequent episodes of violence and aggression that others have described. However, even though outward civility prevailed for the most part, just below the surface and across the spectrum of age and race, layers of resentment and discord held a commanding presence in our school environments.

INTRODUCTION

Memphis in the Meantime

Mississippi River Bridge

In 1972, at age eighteen, I drove away from Memphis, watching its skyline fade in my rearview mirror, with no intention of ever again calling it home.

A jet-black billboard with stark white letters had captured my attention on a trip to Connecticut. It simply said:

That progressive message convinced me to give New England a try. I flat out needed a change. Of course, the Northeast, which I proceeded to call home for twenty years, didn't present itself as the promised land. But I appreciated it for what it was, which wasn't Memphis.

I wouldn't set my sights on the Bluff City again until the spring of 2005, when I traveled from Wyoming with my mom, Sonya, my brother, Bob, and his partner, Susan. Our plans included the Memphis in May BBQ competition and the famed Juke Joint Blues Festival in Clarksdale, Mississippi.

What we didn't anticipate was a very personal and profoundly moving tour of the National Civil Rights Museum. Having been present when Dr. King was killed, the Reverend Billy Kyles spent the rest of his life bearing witness to that event. As it turned out, he was available the weekend we visited Memphis. The man I'd known since the age of thirteen didn't simply walk us through that museum; every room, every exhibit was offered as a personal retrospective. Five hours later we were all famished. True to form, the Reverend invited the bunch of us to his house for lunch and that afternoon found us carrying on as if thirty-five years and a whole lot of water under the proverbial bridge hadn't separated us.

That return to Memphis stirred something in me that was wholly unanticipated. It felt like home. I was transported back to my youth as we stood on the banks of the Mississippi River, heard the familiar rhythm of cicadas, sought shade under waxen leaves of towering magnolia trees and took in the unmistakable sweetness and brilliance of springtime in the South. Even the morning humidity that enveloped us on the front porch as we sipped coffee felt like a good old friend – for a minute.

Magnolia blossom

After a flurry of emails and phone calls, some of my best friends from high school gathered in Memphis that same weekend. Most of us hadn't seen each other for more than thirty years; in a few cases name tags would have been helpful. We found it impossible to condense three decades of life into the hours spent together. When I left the city that time, I knew I'd be back. The place where I'd come of age was still in my blood. My perspective and expectations had changed. As had Memphis.

Two Different Worlds

The landscapes of the Rocky Mountain region and the Mississippi Delta could not represent more starkly different topographies, environments or demographics. I was born in one geographical and political climate and grew up in another; depending on my home base at the time, I have spent many hours over the years traveling to points east or west.

Springtime in Laramie feels like winter in Memphis. Springtime in Memphis feels like heaven, as the mere suggestion of brilliant new growth offers a dreamy sensory experience. March. When showy blossoms whisper the arrival of warmth and outdoor activity. One can wait impatiently each year for spring to arrive in Wyoming, but doing so is a waste of time and hope. It shows up when it's good and ready. June. Even then, snow showers or full-on storms can cruelly postpone the season for a few additional weeks. Locals appease themselves by repeating, "it's okay, we need the moisture." By that time, the South is feelin' it – the heat, that is – and with it, the impending doom of summertime, which lasts almost as long as winter in the Rockies.

Even though we left Wyoming before I turned two, my family roots run deep in Laramie and the nearby mountains where, as a kid, I spent part of each summer. The months that I now spend there each year evoke countless memories and always bring the promise of new adventure.

Memphis, on the other hand, saw me through ten significant years. When I left in 1972, I now understand that I was effectively running away from a lot of heartache and conflict. Once again calling Memphis home has allowed me to face some of that angst and to forge a new reality in a city that is, even with its considerable growth and development, deeply and wonderfully familiar.

As substantively different as the South and the West are in many ways with their localized twists and slants, they do share a spectacular collection of creative souls and adventurers. Every conceivable medium is illuminated by visionary artists. Cooks and chefs reimagine traditional cuisines, while farm to table growers continue to transform Americans' relationship with food. Inspired coffee roasters and craft beer brewers enjoy dedicated followings. Mountain climbers and river rafters cheat death in daring escapades. Gifted singer-songwriters introduce new tunes and cover standards in the intimacy of house concerts. All manner of other professionals and entrepreneurs keep alive the American spirit of individuality and enterprise.

Home on the Range

Located in the southeast corner of Wyoming, Laramie was built on what is known as high plains. The countryside is covered with sagebrush, lined with snow fences and dotted with grazing antelope. Trees come at a premium in much of the state and without that visual obstruction, the sky appears absolutely vast. Mountains remain snow-capped year round due to squalls and storms as late as June and as early as September. Warm sunny days and cool invigorating nights combine for ideal summer seasons, virtually free of insects, humidity or any need for air conditioning. Winters, during which layers of outer wear are critical for survival, bring bitterly low temperatures and wind chills, often well below zero. Incessant winds can whip even an inch of snow cover into white-out conditions, forcing closures of highways and interstates across the state.

Each time zone on this continent enjoys particular rituals and regional peculiarities. The Rocky Mountain region occupies a big swath of this country and, though impossible to corral its people into a single dimension, the whole of it does host a few idiosyncratic norms. In this world, country music tends to rule, cowboys and rodeos are king and cowgirls are tough, able to compete with the best of 'em.

It's a world in which the products of calf castrations, amusingly referred to as Rocky Mountain Oysters, are sometimes eaten freshly harvested and raw at annual branding events. Restaurants throughout Wyoming offer them deep fried. No thank you. Needless to say, not everyone who resides in western states owns a ranch, busts a bronc, raises cattle or consumes such regional delicacies.

Demographically and politically, to describe Wyoming as predominantly Caucasian and conservative would be a gross understatement. As a whole, the state stands proud of its leanings and puts forth great effort to maintain both categorical distinctions. Laramie, however, enjoys a uniquely liberal curve and an ever-so-slightly more diverse population, compliments of the University of Wyoming faculty and student body.

Catfish Blues

On the other hand, Memphis sits atop a river bluff, the states of Mississippi immediately to the south and Arkansas just to the west. In fact, the Tennessee/Arkansas state lines lie in the middle of the Mississippi River. Memphis offers a steamy, lush canvas teeming with a plethora of insects. Spring rains usher in a spectrum of color on redbuds, azaleas, dogwoods and hydrangeas. Cotton, now mechanically planted and harvested, and impossibly flat rice fields abound. Rivers swell, often overflowing their banks as northern snows melt and regional rainfalls collect.

The roiling, muddy waters of the mighty Mississippi at Memphis are a mile wide and seventy feet deep. Summers are sultry, the steady hum of essential air conditioners providing droll background music. Harmonic melodies of smooth rhythm and blues and classic soul tunes spin over the airwaves.

This region survives on smoked and barbecued everything, including but not limited to: deep-fried bologna, pork shoulder and ribs, chicken wings, turkey legs and brisket. In other words, just about anything that ever walked on two legs or four. Even spaghetti is often served with barbeque sauce. Except for health food devotees and the occasional vegetarian, Southerners eat barbecue. Often.

Most southern folks eat catfish too, and a whole lot of it. *Noodling* is a particular form of fishing enjoyed by select grown people in the Delta. It involves wading into muddy creek or river shallows and with bare hands, pulling catfish from their dark hiding places. Good grief. Just as not everyone in western states wrangles cattle, not every Southerner offers his or her bare skin to the gaping jaws of catfish.

Winters can be cold, wet and undeniably miserable in the Mid South area, but are mild and short in comparison to those in the Rockies. When snow falls in Memphis, schools often close and children hope for enough accumulation to sled hillsides or fashion sculptures. Smart drivers know enough to stay off the streets.

As opposed to Laramie, Memphis has a majority Black population and votes overwhelmingly Democratic.

Two very different worlds.

Roots

For the sake of context and background, allow me to shake a few limbs of my family tree:

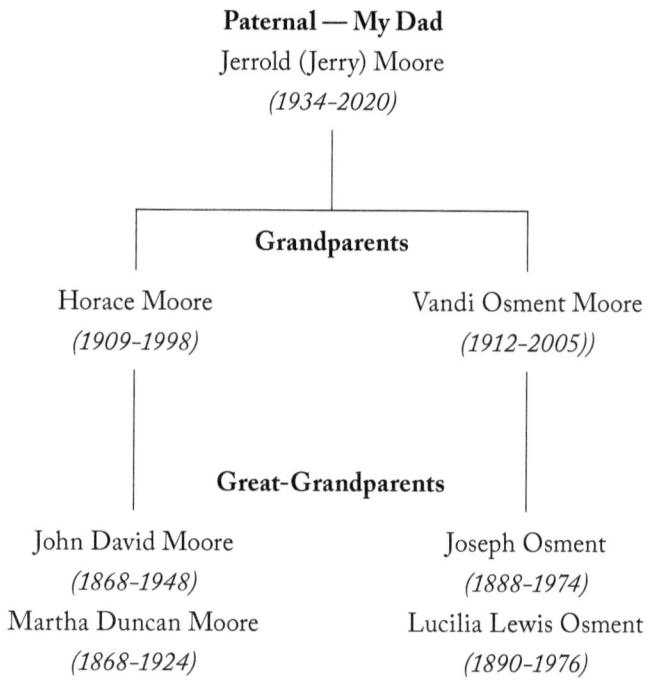

Paternal — My Dad
Jerrold (Jerry) Moore
(1934-2020)

Grandparents

Horace Moore
(1909-1998)

Vandi Osment Moore
(1912-2005))

Great-Grandparents

John David Moore
(1868-1948)
Martha Duncan Moore
(1868-1924)

Joseph Osment
(1888-1974)
Lucilia Lewis Osment
(1890-1976)

Lucilia Lewis and Joseph Osment hailed from northeastern Georgia at a time when desperately poor white and Black folks alike toiled as share-croppers. In a scene that brings to mind Dorothea Lange's photographs of Americans during the Great Depression, my great-grandparents were married by a pastor cousin at a dirt crossroads in the Georgia countryside.

Throughout her life, my great-grandmother, Lucilia, steadfastly maintained her claim of superiority over her "colored" counterparts, even though they all worked the same land, under the same grim conditions. Regardless of where she lived, before turning in at night she looked under her bed for "darkies," who she believed were lying in wait to harm her. Lured by the promise of employment with the Union Pacific Railroad – UPRR – the couple moved west in the 1930's, where Joseph worked as a telegrapher for the railroad in Nebraska and Wyoming.

After their marriage in 1930, Vandi and Horace also transitioned from the deep South to the western plains. Horace was employed as a book-keeper for the UPRR in North Platte, Nebraska and Laramie, Wyoming. Jerry, the older of two children, was born in North Platte in 1934. At age five, he moved with his parents to Wyoming, when his dad transferred to the Laramie railyard. Vandi enjoyed a part time career as a published author and newspaper journalist.

Jerry, 1941   Vandi, Jerry, Horace, 1939

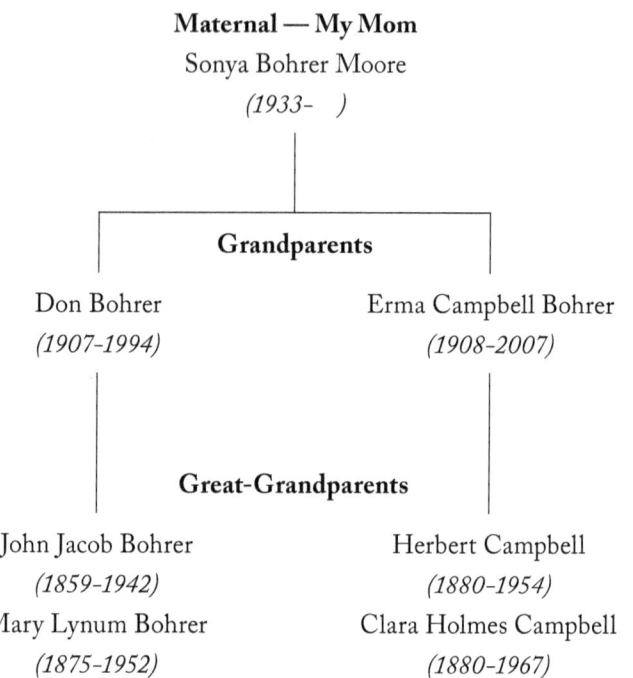

Maternal — My Mom

Sonya Bohrer Moore

(1933-)

Grandparents

Don Bohrer

(1907-1994)

Erma Campbell Bohrer

(1908-2007)

Great-Grandparents

John Jacob Bohrer

(1859-1942)

Mary Lynum Bohrer

(1875-1952)

Herbert Campbell

(1880-1954)

Clara Holmes Campbell

(1880-1967)

The Holmes and Campbells represented a stock of gritty homesteaders and farmers. Herbert and Clara Campbell farmed the land, first in Iowa and later in Missouri, eking out a living by raising chickens, a few beef cattle, a couple head of milk cows and a substantial garden, much of which was either put into cold storage or canned for winter consumption. Establishing our family's early roots in Wyoming around 1910, Clara's brother, Floyd Holmes and his wife, Georgella, claimed a homestead on hardscrabble ground, just north of Cheyenne.

Employed as a young Iowa school teacher, Erma Campbell met her future husband, my grandfather, while visiting her aunt and uncle at their Wyoming homestead. Also drawn to Wyoming to work for the UPRR,

Don found employment in its Cheyenne baggage room. The two soon married and their first child, Sonya, my mother, the oldest of four, was born in their home in August of 1933.

When she was a toddler, the family moved to Laramie, where Don delivered rural route mail for the USPS and remodeled houses. Erma was a dedicated church pianist, cooked the best comfort foods and kept a mean house.

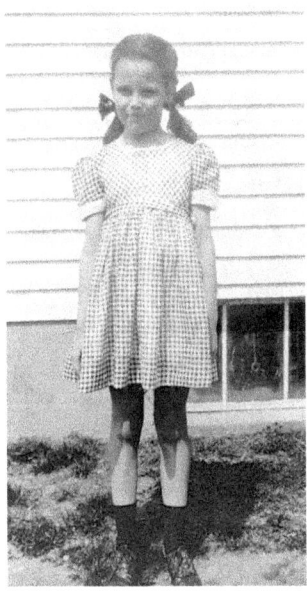 

Sonya, 1940   Don and Erma, 1930

September Song

Jerry and Sonya, wedding day, 1951

This journey down memory lane begins with my parents, Sonya and Jerry, as they are the obvious reason that I'm here. We have shared many miles on this highway of life. Theirs, like mine, were not traditional or predictable trajectories in many ways, either as individuals or as the couple they once were. When they moved away from Laramie in 1956, they couldn't possibly have imagined spending a decade in Memphis. Nor could they have anticipated the ways those years would impact and shadow them, how those memories would echo within them for the rest of their lives.

My parents met in high school at Laramie Prep, the University of Wyoming-affiliated teaching laboratory. They graduated valedictorian of their respective classes, Sonya a year ahead of Jerry.

Prep basketball, Jerry #35

On September 3, 1951, at the beginning of Jerry's senior year of high school, my parents eloped across the state line to Walden, Colorado. Too young to marry in Wyoming at ages seventeen and eighteen, their Colorado wedding raised a few eyebrows in small-town Laramie. After a short courthouse ceremony, the wedding party, including grandparents, parents and siblings, headed for a celebratory picnic in the mountains.

My brother, Bob, born in April of 1952, was in attendance as an infant at Jerry's high school graduation ceremony. Black and white photographs of our parents with their first child frame and document the beginning of their married life. Jerry began his undergraduate studies at the University of Wyoming in the fall of 1952 on a one-year basketball scholarship, a full course load and a part-time job.

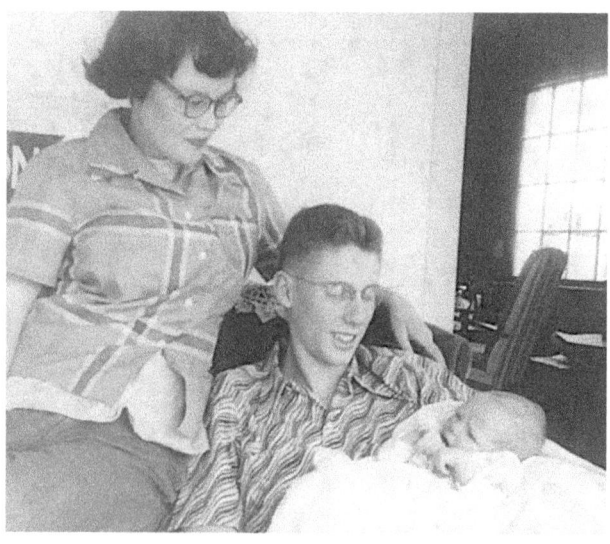

Sonya, Jerry, Bob, 1952

My sister, Melissa (Lissa), and I were quickly added to the family roster in 1953 and 1954, respectively. Having delivered her first two children via caesarean section, Sonya's obstetrician joked that he would have installed a zipper had he known she was going for a third child. My mother had just celebrated her twenty-first birthday when I was born in September of 1954. Still standing is the tiny cottage that we called home. I'm amazed that five of us coexisted under that roof, even given that three of us were very young and very small at the time. These days, families with three kids seem to think that the standard is a five-bedroom house with multiple bathrooms and a three-car garage. Our home consisted of three rooms, including the bathroom.

I can only surmise that sheer fortitude and determination sustained my parents during those early years of marriage. Youthful energy might well have proved their most critical asset as they juggled family life with three babies, school demands and precious little money. As the first grandchildren on both sides, we were beneficiaries of a lot of time and attention from a set of great-grandparents, two sets of grandparents and several aunts and uncles. Hilarious home movies taken by my Grandpa Don include video of me in diapers crawling and later toddling after Bob and Lissa.

A dogged insistence on safeguarding and sustaining western culture has always boasted deep roots. Until fairly recently, young families in the region tended to stay put, finding employment and building futures in their hometowns. My parents, on the other hand, couldn't wait to leave the confines of Laramie. Upon graduation from UW with a Bachelor's Degree in Civil Engineering, Jerry was accepted into a City Planning Masters program at Georgia Tech.

Midnight Train to Georgia

In June of 1956, the five of us said goodbye to a score of family members. Men shook hands and patted backs, teary women and children hugged. Loaded into our two-door Chevy coupe, we drove away from the majestic Rocky Mountains, headed toward the rolling, grassy plains of the midwest, on to the smothering humidity of the Delta and finally to the big city of Atlanta.

That could not have been a pleasant road trip with three youngsters bouncing around the back seat, hot air and cigarette smoke wafting through the car. As the youngest, I was usually sandwiched between my brother and sister, contributing to cruel and unpleasant bouts of motion sickness. Didn't take me long to learn that if I threatened to actually be sick, I'd be granted a place next to my mom on the front seat.

With us went suitcases filled with clothing, while our few household possessions rumbled toward Atlanta in a Union Pacific rail car. Left behind in Laramie were the layers of clothing we needed at 7,200 feet as we headed to an elevation close to sea level and, to say the least, a much warmer climate.

Landing on Luckie Street in a two-story public housing apartment complex, we were met by indecipherable southern drawls and unfamiliar smells emanating from neighbors' kitchens. We were also introduced to unmitigated summer heat with no air conditioning to temper the misery and a Jurassic Park-like community of cockroaches that seemed to be everywhere, especially under bare feet.

Sonya reflects that moving to Atlanta was like entering a foreign country. I'm not sure she felt so "luckie."

Because any furniture we owned traveled by rail, army cots, borrowed from one of Jerry's professors at Georgia Tech, served as temporary beds. With four cots for five people, my imagination places me, youngest and smallest, squarely on a pile of blankets. Our beds must have been a mighty welcome sight when they arrived and were hefted to the two upstairs bedrooms.

The young couple from Wyoming suddenly found themselves in a racially diverse, yet completely segregated city, confronted with arcane inclinations and divides particular to the Deep South. The housing complex that we called home for two years was filled with low income white families like ours. Compared to a three-bedroom apartment next door which housed a family of eleven, our little household probably seemed luxurious. My folks weren't immune to hardship and going without, but the degree of struggle and deprivation that they faced in Atlanta was different. After relying on help from family members in Laramie for years, they now faced new challenges on their own. In so many aspects of daily life, they simply had to make do. For six months, which must have seemed like an eternity, my mom washed our bedding and clothing in the bath-tub – including my cloth diapers – until one of Jerry's colleagues offered her a used wringer-washer. Unable to even afford the price of machines at a nearby laundromat, my parents' limited income demanded that they, quite literally, balance their fixed budget to the penny each month.

Jerry surveyed for the Georgia Highway Department, full-time during summer months and part-time while attending classes. Well-tutored from an early age by her mom, Sonya kept us fed, clothed and otherwise intact. I don't know how my parents endured the stresses of those two years: adjusting to life in an unnervingly strange environment, to the increased demands of time and focus in grad school and to the ever-changing needs of three little ones. We kids didn't know we were poor. Our parents knew how to make ends meet and their frugality served us well. We had what we needed and not much more. They and so many others just did what they had to do, all the while trying to imagine and forge a better life for their families.

Bob, Lissa, Shelley, Atlanta Christmas, 1956

In 2021, the same feelings of desperation, grief and hopelessness that consumed so many hearts and souls during the Depression are once again dominating the lives of far too many Americans who battle the same insecurities — especially during this Covid-19 pandemic. The saddest and most maddening aspect of this crisis is that it didn't have to cripple our country and claim more than half a million lives. Lack of national leadership in the pandemic's early days and a constituency that continues to refuse compliance has allowed the virus to seep into every community in our land and wreak havoc on its people.

Wichita Lineman

Sonya, Lissa, Shelley, Bob, Jerry, Wichita, 1961

As a graduate student, Jerry made the decision to pursue a career in public service. Political office held no interest for him. After receiving his Master's Degree from Georgia Tech in the spring of 1958, he accepted the position of Associate Planning Director for the City of Wichita. Once again, our marginal collection of belongings was shipped, an accumulation that thankfully included dressers and beds, table and chairs. The highway took us northwest to the prairies and rolling grasslands of Kansas, leaving behind the jarring accents and oppressive heat of Atlanta. We were happily headed toward a slightly more familiar part of the country. I was particularly glad that this move would significantly shorten our stifling summer road trips to Wyoming.

We lived in Wichita rentals for the next three years before my parents settled into home ownership of a relatively spacious two-story house on Faulkner Street in 1961. How far they had come from Atlanta public housing. At all of twenty-eight years old, my folks surely felt that they had finally arrived. Two degrees, two moves and three kids later, their perseverance and hard work had begun to pay off handsomely. They were putting down roots with the security of a good job, a nice home and a growing community of friends.

In our free time, we kids were left to our own devices and expected to entertain ourselves. Weather permitting, we were outside and adventurous, barefoot and carefree. I spent hour after hour on the seat of a neighbor's abandoned, rusty tractor, developing a taste for wanderlust with imaginary journeys to faraway places. If housebound, we found plenty of ways to amuse ourselves. Complaining of boredom was simply not an option. Typical siblings, we had our share of spats and telling on each other, but, for the most part, we knew to keep out of our mom's way. There were always chores to be done or bedrooms to stew in if our wells of imagination ran dry.

Memphis, Tennessee

Little did we know that early the following year, after only six months in our spacious new home, a tempting offer would come Jerry's way; the position promised a higher starting salary and a new job description. The overture was flattering and it was enticing, so off my parents went to meet with local officials, to scout housing and schools, to get a feel for the metropolitan area. To decide if Memphis would be our new home.

Not long after their return from the big city on the Mississippi, our Faulkner house went on the market and Jerry gave his notice to the City of Wichita. We packed up yet again and landed in Memphis in June of 1962, three months before my eighth birthday.

We couldn't wait to tell our western family that the City of Memphis had as many residents as the *entire* State of Wyoming: four hundred thousand.

CHAPTER ONE

Walking in Memphis

In the summer of 1962, Jerry started his new job as Planning Director for the City of Memphis, under the leadership of Mayor Henry Loeb. Faced with a family emergency, Loeb stepped away from office in 1963. William Ingram then served as mayor from 1963 to 1967. Mayor Ingram often took exception to Jerry's professional decisions, branding him a "pedigreed outsider." Outsider, fair enough. Pedigreed? Not a chance.

Bob, Shelley, Lissa, Vance Avenue, 1962

Uninterested in buying again right away, my parents signed a lease on a foursquare brick home at 1505 Vance Avenue. Rent on our four-bedroom Midtown home was one hundred seventy-five dollars a month. Good public schools were within walking distance, my folk's church of choice was nearby and the house was situated in, arguably, one of the city's loveliest older neighborhoods. Statuesque trees, old-fashioned street lamps and homes sporting distinctive architecture and unique character provided a charming ambience. There were kids in most of the homes. Families in the general area, now historically designated as Central Gardens, tended to come from blue-blood lines of old-Memphis money. Dads held white-collar jobs and moms managed households and all things kid-related.

The three of us made friends with kids on the block, even though it was clear from the get-go that we didn't share their families' upper middle class standing. All of them were homeowners, while we rented. The interiors of our neighbors' houses were fancier, their cars and clothes were nicer and they all employed maids and yardmen. Parents belonged to country clubs and organizations of status and wealth. Their children attended private schools and elite summer camps. But, we were kids and kids can be tempted by the sweetness of privilege. Besides, they were my new friends. I wasn't about to turn down excursions to country club pools, lake houses or beach hotels to find respite from the dog days of summer.

I was clearly seen as fresh fodder for several women on our street, who set out to initiate me into their genteel environment of southern exposure and tradition. I was tutored in the importance of good posture, the art of needlepoint and the correct way to eat a steamed artichoke, my first. I even learned to water ski, no small feat for a Wyoming girl. Perhaps the most pertinent lesson was the insistence that adults be addressed as "ma'am" and "sir." When I understood that this practice of address was non-negotiable, the titles soon rolled off my tongue like warm sorghum molasses. It may surprise Southerners to learn that those terms of respect aren't used by most Americans on a regular basis.

My ear initially struggled with regional colloquialisms, made even more alien by the accents with which they were issued. I could've used a Delta dictionary, complete with a pronunciation guide.

"All ya'll come in for dinner."

"You kids are gettin' on my last nerve!"

"Your new friend is cute as a bug's ear."

"Gimme some sugar before you leave."

"She tumped over in the swing."

"My mom's fit to be tied."

Bob, Lissa and I went to public schools while most of the other kids on our street were enrolled in private academies. Defined by their socio-economic status, our neighbors were dropped off at the same schools that for decades had educated many of their family members.

Women in our neighborhood were involved in charitable community efforts and country club activities. Theirs was a life of relative leisure, a traditional role for white southern women of means. They were expected to marry young, bear children, support their husbands and guide their families through the routines of daily life and social connections. Dressed in flowing caftans, women on Vance Avenue could be seen strolling between houses on warm evenings, cocktails in hand. If my mother thought Atlanta was a foreign environment, our Memphis neighborhood must have felt like an alternate universe.

Is It True What They Say About Dixie?

"As a woman in the South at that time, you either had a maid or you were one." – Anonymous

The meat of the housework and child rearing in many, if not most, southern white households was done by Black women. Maids. Domestics. The help. There were families that chose not to or couldn't afford to employ maids. But in that decade and ones previous, the above generalization held true for most white homes within the middle and upper class socio-economic strata of Midtown Memphis.

This servitude sometimes saw wealthy white girls sent off to school with a personal maid. I've often wondered: Where did the displaced Black women live? To what extent and in what ways did they serve their young charges? What were they paid for their sacrifice and labor? And, most importantly, who did they leave behind?

In my late teens I needed a job, which really meant I needed some spending money. Looking through the local want ads, most of the jobs offered to women were on the domestic front. Maids. Truth be told, there was an element of intrigue in my pursuit, but I also really did need a job. I knew enough about house cleaning by that point in my life, and what I didn't know, I could surely fudge. Using our sturdy black rotary phone, I started calling the numbers listed.

"Honey, are you a white girl?"

"Yes, ma'am, I am."

"Oh, we only hire colored maids."

After placing several phone calls with the same outcome, I realized that I wouldn't even be granted an interview. My first waitressing job awaited me. Days of overt slavery were gone, but in truth, not much had changed in the dynamics, economic realities and social order between white and Black citizens. There was no doubt that white folks remained on top and in charge. As they mowed and trimmed, raked and swept, harvested and hauled, pressed and shined, most Black southerners labored to ease white folks' burdens. Every maid, every yard man and every garbage man in Memphis was Black, each performing essential work in exchange for obscenely low wages.

When Will We Be Paid?

Dear Mattie,

You are the first Black woman I've ever known. In pristine white uniforms and worn shoes, you work in a house across the street from us. Five long days a week, riding a series of city buses to and from work, you leave your own children in the care of your mother. I know that you're never picked up or dropped off at your house, but sometimes when it's raining, the lady you work for fetches you from the bus stop. Every time, I watch you climb into or out of the back seat of her car. Always the back seat. You have dedicated your waking hours to the well-being of that white family and I'll bet they don't even know your kids' names or where you live.

I hear talk that you and other maids make three dollars a day for all the cleaning, cooking, ironing and childcare you do. What you are paid is not what you have earned.

Sometimes I eat dinner in that house across the street. You cook and serve the meal, then eat alone in the kitchen. Every dining room on our street has a buzzer built into the floor, used to summon the help, just like the one Queen Elizabeth uses to call or dismiss her servants. Our house has a buzzer, but no maid and most certainly no Queen. At day's end, you wearily trudge back to the bus stop to begin your long journey home. To take care of your own.

I like to hang out with you while you're ironing and watching soaps. We talk some about your kids. Mostly we don't talk, but I don't think you mind me sitting with you. The other day, outside the kitchen where you were working, I stepped on a big nail in my bare feet. You hushed my screaming, calmly sat with me on the door stoop, and pulled that rusty eight penny straight out of my foot. A few days before that, I fell out of my friend's hammock,landing hard on bare ground. Laughing, you picked me up, made sure I wasn't hurt, dusted me off, and sent me back to playing.

Once a week, a Black man slowly pushes a big ol' cart loaded with seasonal crops down our street. I love sitting on the curb, listening to you and the farmer as you pull out allotted grocery money and buy tomatoes, melons or cucumbers for the white family. I've never seen anything like it. Not the farmer selling his wares, not how you joke and laugh with each other.

I can tell that you really love the four kids in that house across the street. They're your "babies." You've raised them like your own, and they know you're in charge when their mama's not around. When they're naughty, you tell them "go outside and get me a switch! You're fixin' to get a lickin'!" I kind of don't get this whole situation, but I know better than to get crossways with you.

I'm sorry you have to leave your young kids at home and I don't understand why you have to work so hard for so little pay. Why don't those people do their own housework and punish their own kids? Still, I'm really glad that I get to see you most days.

One day I think I'll appreciate my front-row seat in all of this and understand what I was witnessing. When I'm older, I'll surely have a different perspective on the age-old intersection of Black lives and white privilege.

SEM

I Love a Parade

Everett R. Cook, the President of the Memphis Cotton Exchange, said this:

"Carnival is to promote business for everybody and should not be used by any one group. It is for all of the stores and all of the people, for all kinds of professions and businesses, for the city as a whole, regardless of the size of the business, the social standing, wealth, prestige, family background or anything else that would tend to make anyone feel that he or she would not be invited to participate in Carnival."

As wonderfully inclusive as that sounds, what he left out was this:

"Unless you're Black."

The Memphis Cotton Carnival Association failed to include the city's Black population in its invitation to the annual party. This, despite the fact that an upper echelon of white landowners had long enjoyed staggering riches made off the backs and from the shredded, bloodied fingers of Black cotton pickers. People like to say, "Well, that's just the way it was back then." Actually, "the way it was" amounted to nothing less than a willful and intentional refusal to embrace and acknowledge the very humanity and dignity of an entire race of people. There was no legal basis for the segregation that defined the Cotton Carnival. That's simply how things worked in the South. Just the way it was.

Each spring, a middle-aged man of wealth, prestige and social connection was selected by a secret committee to reign as Carnival King for the annual festivity. On his arm throughout the season of lavish parties was the Carnival Queen, a very young debutante of high social standing. Family bloodlines of wealthy white Memphians ran deep through Carnival royalty.

To kick off the gala, crowds gathered downtown to watch a luminous and bedecked river barge dock at the cobblestone landing. With great pomp and circumstance, the royal assemblage disembarked and climbed aboard ornate coaches. To the glee of onlookers, a procession of carriages and festive floats ambled along the length of Main Street. Posh and exclusive parties in the city's grand hotels awaited the King and Queen and their coterie.

The Cotton Carnival's elaborate carriages had traditionally been horse-drawn. That is, until someone proposed replacing the animals with human bodies. The very people who weren't invited to the party.

My mind's eye imagines a light bulb moment in a sick comic strip. It goes something like this:

"Hey! Instead of horses, let's use Colored boys to pull the Carnival carriages through downtown! People will love it!"

As contrived and preposterous as this system of using human beings as beasts of burden may sound today, so it went, documented by numerous historical photographs.

In the mid-1930s, R.Q. Venson, a Black dentist with a Beale Street address, disregarded the accepted rules of festival segregation and took a nephew to watch the Carnival parade as it made its way along Main Street. When asked if he liked what he had seen, the young man said,

"No, I didn't. The only Negroes I saw were horses."

That experience spurred the doctor to establish a counterpart to run concurrently with the Cotton Carnival. The Cotton Maker's Jubilee became a celebration of Black peoples' notable and inestimable contributions to the success of the cotton industry. The separate carnival chose its own King, Queen and royalty, hosted a parade on Beale Street and held a round of parties.

For each annual celebration, tens of thousands of dollars were spent on the bling and finery, largely funded by the participants themselves. As a young girl, I was enthralled by the Disney-esque opulence of the sweeping gowns worn by queens and princesses, featured on the morning paper's front page and brought to life on the local evening news.

However, my perspective on the city celebration began to change when I grew old enough to babysit youngsters on our street whose parents, dressed to the nines in formal attire, set out to attend a series of exclusive parties for Memphis' white elite. I started appreciating the absurdity of grown men and women, commoners, claiming royal status and joining secret societies. I also began to question the reasoning behind a set of intentionally separate, very segregated events, all designed to commemorate the same industry.

During the week-long celebrations, the vast majority of the city's Black and white residents were relegated to curbsides. Mere subordinates, they were left to pretend that, in some obscure way, the majestic roll-out held some connection to their daily lives. Then again, everybody loves a parade.

The Cotton Carnival, "The South's Greatest Party," complete with its societal imperfections and exclusions, offered quite an insight into Memphis' racial and economic landscapes for over half a century. Today, Carnival and Jubilee celebrations remain segregated and involve exclusive parties and charitable fundraising.

Something's Happening Here

Every public space in Memphis was segregated in the early 1960s. Although the courts were beginning to rule against the time-honored presumptions and cruel exclusions of separate but equal, Memphis found ways to circumvent the law.

When the order came down to desegregate public facilities, citing repair and maintenance issues, the city immediately closed every public swimming pool for a number of years. That callous decision left thousands of families with no place to find respite from the consuming heat and humidity of summer months.

A black and white photograph taken by Ernest Withers documents the imposing sign posted on Thursdays at the Zoo's front gate:

"No White People Allowed in Zoo Today"

The rest of the week, the Zoo was *only* open to the white public.

City parks, libraries, neighborhoods, places of worship and schools were segregated. As was seating in restaurants and bus and train stations. Movie theaters required Black patrons to use side or back entrances and, once inside, to sit in the balcony. Neither the Board of Education nor city government had Black representation.

But even as Jim Crow laws prevailed, there arose an undeniable drumbeat of change, steadily growing in tempo and timbre. Black leadership, led by Dr. Martin Luther King Jr. and others, organized ever-increasing numbers to resist, march, demonstrate and boycott for civil rights, for fair access to a better quality of life. Although the Constitution and federal law granted those rights to every American, the reality on the ground was another story. That polarity was being unmasked in towns and cities across the South and Memphis was on the map.

Stop, Look and Listen

Conjuring images of controversial patterns of segregation and inequality makes us uncomfortable – regardless of our personal vantage point or set of experiences. For some, those reminders demand that we never forget, that we connect the dots between past and present. For others, the discomfort signals that it's time to simply move on.

The distinct and pervasive racial divide that our family witnessed as we settled into life in Memphis was a sobering introduction to what centuries of slavery had wrought in the Deep South. In the sense that we represented a young, professional white family, we appeared to conform. But, actually, the clearly defined, well-established and strongly defended lifestyles and norms of the Deep South were antithetical to who my parents were and how they chose to live.

Without boast or swagger, this was life in the Moore household: we did not employ a maid or yard man. Ever. In our new environment, we were outliers. True to our working class background, we continued to do the tedious and dirty work which, for us, was simply part of life. We did the dishes and hung laundry on the clothesline, the basketful of resulting ironing seeming to reproduce at will. We cut the lawn with a push mower and cleaned our house every Saturday. The daily and weekly chores were not always done cheerfully, but trust me, they got done. For a quarter, we kids even had the privilege of polishing our dad's dress shoes or the delight of exchanging that quarter for candy or a cherry Coke at Wiles Drug Store on Union Avenue.

When the city could no longer legally justify the closures, pools were finally reopened. Our neighbors watched with disbelief as we, decked out in swimsuits, piled into our Chevy wagon. They knew good and well that we were headed for the recently reopened and newly desegregated Fairgrounds facility. Just happy for the opportunity to spend a hot summer's day in cold water, it didn't matter one whit to us who shared the pool. We were all there for the same good reason.

How and why my parents organically evolved into liberally progressive people remains a question that will probably never be satisfactorily answered. They claim that there was no intellectual or academic exercise involved in the evolution of their socio-political beliefs and related lifestyle. It's simply who they were and how they raised their children.

There was no family mission statement about who we would welcome into our lives and into our home. We kids understood and were witness to the fact that our door was open to everyone, regardless of race, nationality, religious belief, sexual orientation or political leaning.

That was a big deal in Memphis, Tennessee in the 1960s.

Once again, we found ourselves in the deep South but we were clearly not of it.

Bob Moore
Central High School
Class of 1970

For most of us, growing up contains experiences in exploration and exasperation; fulfillment and rejection; acceptance and humiliation. Lessons of love and hatred; bullying and the formation of character. Much of this took place for him in a southern city where he felt an outsider's misery after the comforts of an early life in a familiar and comfortable geography. That city was Memphis in the early 1960s.

Life was simple and sheltered as a very young boy, first in Laramie, then during two years in Atlanta while his dad attended Georgia Tech. The family's quarters in public housing was Deep-South segregated and there were few times when people of color were present in his world. In 1958, a move was made to the plains of Kansas, followed by a return to the South in 1962.

Children have no choice in the moves their parents make. The first shocks were unrelieved heat and humidity after spending a summer on a Wyoming ranch where the heat was dry, cut only by an occasional freezing rain and hail thunderstorm. There were more Black people on the streets and in the markets in Memphis than he'd ever experienced, but as he would soon find, not in the public schools he'd attend. At least not for several years. His first in-your-face racist, segregation moment came as a naive ten-year-old when he drank samples from Coloreds Only/Whites Only water fountains, judging them to have no difference in taste or temperature. Hmmm, what the hell was that all about?

Bob, Laramie, 1969

By his recollection, there was hardly ever any casual or explicit talk among family members about people who were not like them – people of color or people who spoke differently. However, there was the Georgia-born grandmother who took a number of years to torturously thread her way from "nigra" to "Negro" to "Black." There was no particular lesson in his upbringing of people

53

being "other" or classified as lesser human beings. The integration of white schools represented nothing extraordinary to him, while white friends and acquaintances who had been raised in Memphis were quite uncomfortable and considered their lives upended and threatened. His world, however, began changing, in no particular order, with school, athletics and girls. Friends and acquaintances of color would be formed from his three-legged stool that ruled his young life through the end of high school.

With school integration and the assassination of Dr. King, school-sanctioned social traditions like homecoming dances and proms were eliminated. Athletic games between his integrated high school and the still all-Black schools were moved from evenings to afternoons. Socially integrated occasions were parties held at friends' houses, highlighting the good times in smaller gatherings, experiencing what the rest of his classmates were missing with the elimination of school customs. There were also times of naive adventure. After city buses stopped their routes for the night, walking down Beale Street toward home didn't worry him. Nor did the thrilling risk of a carful of white and Black teens going to the drive-in and the possible consequences of being pulled over by white police officers.

His family was as involved in the social, political and cultural dynamics of the city as many other families and individuals were; perhaps more so because his father, Jerry Moore, was first hired as Senior City Planner in 1962 and then appointed the city's Chief Administrative Officer in 1968. It was in these two positions that he helped direct infrastructure maintenance and improvement in city departments. He also tracked budget and policy, updating the City Council at its meetings. It was a time of crisis and consequence in City Hall and on the streets of Memphis.

One of the most egregious examples of segregation was the Memphis Cotton Carnival and the Cotton Makers Jubilee, both established during the Great Depression. The Carnival celebrated white society while the Jubilee embraced Black contributions to the dominant economic engine through the 1960s.

The power structure in the city ensured that the two cultures, segregated by skin color, would not celebrate together; each group held its own parades and soirees. This week-long event that echoed many aspects of Mardi Gras took place every May and was a masked disguise of the fear most white folk had for their Black neighbors.

On the other side of this was the late winter evening he spent as one of a small handful of white folk in a sanctuary of Black hope and expectation. The crowd listened to Dr. King while funds were raised in support of the striking sanitation workers. It would be the next-to-last time the Black leader, a living illustration of peaceful activism, would stand with this group of people.

As shifts in society were occurring, including demands to change the dominant order of white patriarchy and racism, so too was his consciousness growing; from naive acceptance of the world as it was to the possibilities of shared lives and better circumstances for all. Years later, his days in Memphis from 1962 to 1970 have come to represent, not without pain or regret, a struggle from the cocoon of ease and complacency into an adulthood that sees us all as humans related by everything we hold in common.

Irony also has a place in this story. The time period from the early 1950s through the 1970s found Black and white folk gathering in the Memphis studios of Sun, Stax, Hi, American and Ardent to create some of the most phenomenal music on the planet. This young man was aware of the music because it was broadcast on his tiny AM 9-volt radio, but he was not conscious of it being birthed a couple of miles from his house. It took leaving the city, never returning to live, to appreciate the gifts those musicians left to us in color-blind collaborations. It had all happened with his mind fixed in other directions. Today he tries to pay this musical legacy forward by highlighting Memphis and southern music on his two weekly Wyoming public radio programs. They are broadcast statewide as well as world-wide, thanks to online streaming.

Sun Studio, Memphis

CHAPTER TWO

Good Morning, School Girl

Shelley, 1961

September of 1962 saw my siblings and me enrolled at Idlewild Elementary School. Established in 1903 and still ranked as one of Memphis' finest, Idlewild remains a midtown institution, a looming brick structure with a commanding presence on an otherwise quiet residential street. The parents and grandparents of some of our new classmates had been educated at Idlewild.

While a few of our teachers were young and enthusiastic, others mirrored the matronly sobriety of its principal, Miss Imelda Stanton. The unrivaled matriarch of Idlewild, she was the living caricature of a short, stocky old-maid school teacher, complete with yellow-white hair spiraled in tight pin curls. A strict disciplinarian, she employed a wooden ruler ready to rap the knuckles of anyone unfortunate enough to be sent to her office. Thankfully, I never got whacked by her but I heard plenty of kids recount their tearful sessions with Miss Stanton.

School buildings back in the day weren't air conditioned. When classes commenced in September, we endured lingering heat and humidity, making third-floor classrooms especially unbearable. Come fall, radiators were turned on for the duration of winter months, bringing their own steamy oppression to our interminably long school days until we could once again welcome springtime and the promise of summer vacation.

In Kansas, we had learned the Cold War ritual of "duck and cover," somehow convinced by our teachers that school desks would actually protect us from incoming Soviet missiles. In a similar vein, as young Idlewild students, we donned matching sashes and caps and marched on the playground to the strains of The Ballad of the Green Beret. I'm sure that we felt quite important as we stepped left-right-left, but we clearly had no idea who we were honoring or why. I can't conjure images of elementary students in 2021 being required to participate in war-themed playacting. These exercises seem not only harmless but almost laughable when compared to today's practice of school lockdowns against armed shooters. From the abstract to the horrifically real. What a world!

As soon as I discovered "chapter books" in the Idlewild library, I found myself drawn to biographies, especially those of girls and women such as Amelia Earhart, Sacajawea, Annie Oakley – frankly, stories that I could insert myself into or otherwise found relatable. Our selections were sorely limited. How I wish that my generation of grade schoolers had been exposed to the greater world through literature and comprehensive history lessons; accurate, inclusive and compelling narratives about accomplished women and men, be they artists, authors, civil and human rights leaders, inventors, musicians, politicians, explorers or everyday heroes. Historical figures representing a range of ethnicities and nationalities. And, to say the least, a much more complete and accurate picture of American history.

Today, my two older grandchildren, Viva and Wolf, are growing up with depths and breadths of awareness that I could never have imagined at their young ages. Their school communities embrace students with varying abilities, skin tones and family structures. They include recent immigrants who are now proud to call America home. My grandkids understand that the United States is a dynamic and complex melting pot of nationalities, traditions and cultures. Their student bodies look like the United Nations of Youth.

In January of her kindergarten year, 2012, my granddaughter, Viva, and her class studied Dr. King's legacy as they celebrated his birthday. Her teacher invited me to share stories of the civil rights icon, including details of his final days in Memphis. I also told of my father's role in that piece of history. Tailoring my stories to meet the minds of six-year-olds was challenging, yet what a remarkable full-circle moment for me.

I was nine when President Kennedy was assassinated in November of 1963. The skies over Memphis were ominously dark and foreboding that afternoon when the unimaginable news came over our school's loudspeaker that the President had been shot. Televisions that typically brought Betty Mothershed's science instruction into classrooms were wheeled out, becoming our information source as the day's updates grew more grim by the hour. Before school was dismissed for the day, we were informed that the President had died. I'd never witnessed such sadness in adults. This was my first cognitive experience with real tragedy, one that would unfortunately be repeated all too often in the ensuing years.

On a much lighter note, my proudest moment at Idlewild involved winning the school spelling bee as a fifth grader. I felt smart as a whip with my crowning as Queen Bee, sparkling sash and all. That fifteen minutes of fame and giddy excitement ended swiftly and embarrassingly several weeks later in the city-wide contest when I misspelled my very first word – which I've conveniently forgotten. Obviously, correctly spelling the word "muscle" to take the Idlewild prize didn't automatically qualify me for successfully competing on the bigger stage.

I did well enough in school, enjoying the rhythm and predictability of the days and weeks. Those were my days of pure innocence and naivete. Competitions in hopscotch, bike riding and jumping rope filled my outdoor hours. Inside, endless board and card games and exactly one hour of nightly television kept me entertained. Weekends with friends were freewheeling after Saturday chores were done.

Walking to and from school with kids who lived on nearby streets took the tedium out of the daily treks. Idlewild saw me through sixth grade, pretty happy in my little bubble, oblivious for the most part to the sweeping changes that were impacting so many lives in my city.

Idlewild Elementary School

The Reverend Julie Allen Berger
Central High School
Class of 1972

Julie in elementary school

My dad's mother, whom we called "Mimi," was a spitfire who liked to dress up, travel, attend "club" gatherings and host us wherever she was living for boisterous family holiday meals.

When I was a girl, she strongly encouraged, i.e., pressured my parents to enroll me and my siblings in one of the organizations closest to her heart. It was the "United Daughters of the Confederacy." The division for kids was "Children of the Confederacy."

I'm not privy to the conversations that went on between my parents about this issue behind closed doors. They were committed to the civil rights struggle and I know they were not enthused about their children being part of this group that was in love with the Confederacy. The upshot? Mimi apparently signed us up as members of the "C of C" without my parents' permission. They compromised by letting things play out without making a scene.

We kids hated the meetings, which involved memorizing a catechism about the proud and misunderstood Confederate States. One time, our grandmother cajoled me into attending a "C of C" convention in Nashville. The main thing I remember is having to dress up for some kind of fancy dinner with a bunch of older women wearing sashes across their chests – and the novelty of staying in a downtown hotel with my cousin. I hated the dressing up part the most, the boring speeches second. This took place in my older elementary years. If I was uncomfortable with the message of the convention, I couldn't yet distill it or verbalize it.

At best, I looked upon all this activity as goofy, kind of like entering a closet housing clothes in mothballs. It seemed benign, which, when I think back, is the scariest part of all. In the last decade I have learned that organizations like "United Daughters of the Confederacy" were part of the "Lost Cause" movement, responsible for placing civil war statues in a number of southern towns. The messages of these statues, I realize now with chagrin, were anything but benign. They were a clear message of "stay in your place," or worse, to people of color.

My younger sister tells me she never attended a "C of C" meeting and yet, while in high school, was elected as state treasurer of the chapter! Our grandmother had secretly submitted her name and, without being present, my sister was voted in. It was at this point that my parents put their feet down. From that time on, there was no more pressure from Mimi for us kids to participate in the "C of C." Yet I, my brother and sister and cousins collectively held our breath when the removal of Jefferson Davis' statue in downtown Memphis was scheduled. We knew our names were inscribed in the base as part of the organization which funded that statue.

In the last two decades, I have recognized more and more my privilege as part of a large, well-connected Memphis family. I have begun to see that my family's standard of living rested very much on generational resources inherited by my parents, my mother especially. My ability to live in a large old house, take ballet, piano and flute lessons as a girl, go to camp and attend a liberal arts college were opportunities many of my classmates did not have. It was not about smarts or hard work. These were opportunities which came my way because we knew the right people and how to take advantage of perks – such as my professor father's sabbatical summer in Europe with his family when I was in high school.

Points of pride for me growing up were knowing that some ancestors on my mother's side had notoriety in American history. One relative deserted the British army to become George Washington's personal surgeon. Another relative connects us to the explorer, Meriwether Lewis. While I am still proud to know this heritage, it is now a clouded pride. I am aware that many Americans do not know their history because their ancestors were enslaved people upon whose labor my ancestors profited.

People Get Ready

There are three Black students in our 1965 combined class photo of eighty-two fifth and sixth graders. At that time, it didn't occur to me to have an opinion on the subject of school desegregation. Kids were kids. I now understand that those first Black students at Idlewild weren't afforded the luxury of such indifference. What I didn't know as well is that they were but three of a number of young Black children in Memphis who, for the first time in their lives, suddenly found themselves surrounded by a veritable sea of white people. Some of us white students were simply unmindful of the significance of Black kids in the classrooms. Others' responses weren't quite as innocuous. If you, as a white reader, don't think this was a big deal, flip the script and put yourself in the Black students' position for just one minute.

Mandatory school desegregation had, on paper, been the law of the land since the U.S. Supreme Court's *Brown Vs. Board of Education* ruling in 1954. But, as was the case with the City of Memphis swimming pools, the local Board of Education found ways to avoid and delay full compliance with the law. In order to mollify government mandates, the Board crafted the low bar definition of "integration" as any school with one enrolled minority student. Let me reiterate: the Memphis School Board deemed that the presence of one Black student in an otherwise white student body constituted an integrated school. Finally bowing to growing pressure from local organizations and the Federal Government, the city was demographically plotted and sectioned in order to determine which Black students would be ferried by city bus or family car to new schools.

The Memphis School Board began implementing the following de-segregation plan: Grades 1-3 were to be desegregated at the beginning of the 1961-62 school year. One grade level would follow suit each succeeding year. Under this plan, it ultimately took a full decade to desegregate Memphis public schools. As a point of clarity, federally mandated busing wasn't enforced in Memphis until January of 1973.

When public school desegregation seemed unavoidable, kids in our neighborhood and thousands of their white peers, already safely embedded in private schools, were joined by a tidal wave of new enrollees. It was clear that vast numbers of Memphis' white population had no appetite for racially integrated school environments for their children. Could it really be that no one anticipated the likelihood of extensive white flight from city schools, if not from the city itself?

Ain't Gonna Let Nobody Turn Me Around

Just across Midtown from Idlewild was another Memphis icon, Bruce Elementary School. In 1961, anticipating the inevitable, Bruce Elementary and three other historically white elementary schools took the cautious, calculated step of enrolling a small number of Black first graders. That group of students came to be known as the Memphis 13. Some of those thirteen students were enrolled in majority-white schools by activist parents who chose to put their families on the front lines of the movement toward school desegregation. Other parents simply believed that their kids would receive a better education in a predominantly white school. For some, it was perhaps a bit of each.

Although hailed as pioneers in the push for equal opportunity, the Memphis 13 speak today to the trauma of suddenly finding themselves in a distinctly minority position with overwhelming public scrutiny. Were these kids really expected to fall into line, to quietly and cheerfully assimilate into a totally new and unfamiliar environment? According to them, that's not what happened. Ignored, teased, bullied and threatened, their individual recollections tell of varied, layered and sometimes conflicting experiences. Some express regret for their place in history, feeling that the personal price they paid was not worth the intended or assumed benefits. Others are proud to have been among those who led the way for inclusiveness in Memphis public schools. Each one of them acknowledges the challenges she or he faced every school day. At least one of the thirteen returned to his neighborhood school, unwilling to endure the cruelty at Bruce Elementary.

There are numerous images of those tiny Black first graders being escorted into their respective new schools by family members, surrounded by a host of armed white police officers – purportedly on site to instill into the situation a sense of order and protection. Little people, asked to personally risk so much in order to pave the way for others. Indeed, asked to change the very tenets of public education in Memphis.

The sudden and unexpected presence of thirteen young Black children in classrooms filled with an overwhelming majority of white kids was not a slam dunk in the process of desegregating Memphis schools. Nevertheless, the quiet rollout was touted as a great success by local, state, even national leaders, all of whom had keenly and purposely withheld details of the plan from the media. Their goal was to at least postpone a predictable groundswell of public protest and outcry from the white community.

Other than limited newspaper articles with photos and spotty local television coverage, I wouldn't become fully aware of what was transpiring on the west side of Midtown until I entered Bellevue Junior High in 1966. Not only were we seventh graders entering a new and unfamiliar academic framework; most of us were also, for the first time, being introduced to a notably racially diverse environment.

What's Going On

For the most part, Black and white kids in the South had never spent time together, anywhere, in any context, under any circumstance. We may have passed each other on downtown sidewalks or in grocery stores as we shopped with our moms, but contemplating the shared spaces of hallways, bathrooms, classrooms, locker rooms, playgrounds and cafeterias was an altogether new dimension. Those uncomfortable with the emergence of school desegregation must have felt like they were walking onto a minefield.

Bellevue Junior High School

Within the walls of majority-white schools, Black and white students were now part of a grand experiment, ostensibly to begin to right the wrongs of so many years of separate and unequal. In boardrooms, courtrooms and living rooms, adults made the decisions and dictated the terms. We children became pawns in a brand new game, being asked to do that which most adults, in their own personal and professional lives, found incomprehensible. The onus was on us as young people to make this groundbreaking clinical trial succeed.

At the onset of desegregation, no attempt was made by school administrators or teachers to provide counsel or guidance through the transition.

In fact, it was pretty obvious that most teachers and administrators were themselves equally unprepared for what lay ahead, with no precedent to follow, no game plan or notes to reference, no seasoned colleagues to consult.

The rulings of the courts were treated as subjective, if not voluntary, by many southern school boards. What follows is a brief accounting of how the City of Memphis dealt with those guidelines and some of the consequences of its decisions.

The Supreme Court's rulings mandated desegregation of the nation's public schools, which meant that state and city governments, school boards, administrators and teachers were faced with how best to comply. The overwhelming consensus among those bodies was that white schools provided superior educational opportunities. Even if that could be proven untrue, the implicit understanding was that white kids would not desegregate Black schools in an effort to balance the scales.

Black schools in Memphis suffered – and largely still do suffer – from the lack of political will to provide equitable and adequate funding and resources. As a result, every aspect of education has been negatively impacted: from facilities and textbooks, technology and equipment, to exposure and opportunity for their students.

Black kids made up half of Memphis' student population in the 1960s, yet there was no one on the School Board to reflect, represent or directly address that community's distinct voices, needs or concerns. The introduction of a relatively small number of Black students into majority-white schools set a terribly low bar for equalizing the educational experience for all Memphis public school students, merely putting a patch on a much deeper wound and a complicated history.

By 1966, with stunted efforts at compliance to desegregate, fewer than 3% of the 65,000 Black students in Memphis were enrolled in white schools. Although those numbers would increase over the years, there was no comprehensive commitment to providing a truly equitable education for the vast majority of Black students in Memphis public schools.

The process of desegregation as we know it ended up being a disappointing, poorly executed, short-sighted and ultimately failed exercise. As I've stated, the Memphis school board did only the bare minimum required, the members' hearts and minds clearly not invested in the process, its purpose or its outcome.

The mass exodus of white students from public to private schools over a period of several years was the linchpin in upending that plan. The white student population in Memphis city schools, some 65,000 kids, steadily dwindled by 20,000 during the early years of desegregation. By the beginning of the 1973-1974 school year, almost half of the remaining 45,000 white students had transitioned to segregated private academies.

CHAPTER THREE

The First Time Ever I Saw Your Face

My peers and I lived through – in fact embodied – the transition to desegregated schools. We witnessed the good, the bad and the ugly of that march, however imperfect, toward greater equality. We were given a tremendous opportunity to expand our horizons in ways that went far beyond lessons in the classroom. Though not always pretty or comfortable years, for those of us open to new possibilities, they were critically important chapters in our adolescent development.

Most kids' lives change exponentially when they move into middle school. Bellevue would prove to be an even more dynamic experience altogether. The tectonic plates of my personal world shifted and expanded into entirely unexpected new dimensions as I moved through seventh, eighth and ninth grades, when my sheltered Dick-and-Jane narratives got turned on their ears.

Watching my sister and brother advance to junior high school, I listened with awe and a bit of trepidation as they talked about changing classes, more demanding schoolwork and a much larger student body. Having reached the top of the game as a sixth grader at Idlewild, I would again be relegated to the bottom rung of the ladder as a seventh grader. My concerns were pretty basic and predictable: how would I ever navigate the hallways to find my next classroom before the bell rang? Would I be able to keep up with the school work, the new sets of expectations from various teachers? Would friendships hold over from Idlewild as we entered junior high?

I was in the unenviable but familiar role of following two bright siblings into Bellevue. Seventh grade teachers knew who I was and who preceded me, which would prove to be either a blessing or a curse for all three of us during our years there. Bob and Lissa, who generally played by the rules, undoubtedly shuddered as I inched toward, shall we say, a tendency to coloring outside the lines, a proclivity for getting into "good trouble."

There was a sense that some white teachers and students at Bellevue who had the luxury of staying put wanted to just get on with it, hoping to block out or ignore as much of the chatter as possible. But, the sudden presence of Black students in hallways and classrooms clearly threatened a previously tidy, predictable, homogeneous world .

Seeing Black teachers at the front of the classroom was a new experience for most of us white kids. For Black students in a majority-white environment, teachers who looked like them were surely a welcome sight. As is always the case, some Bellevue teachers were better than others. The good ones were exceptionally good. They made us better students. Today, when we former classmates talk about those years, most of us agree that if one paid attention and did the work there was a whole lot of learning to be had at Bellevue.

Adding to the complexity of the racial dynamic was the typical range of diversity within the student body as a whole. As in any public school environment, Bellevue's enrollment included mediocre students and high achievers, kids from the projects and those from middle and upper class homes, kids who toed the line and those who bore the stigma of being purported "troublemakers."

No matter their status within the school community, Black students were asked, implicitly or explicitly, to conform to the norms of established white culture. From my perspective, there is simply no other way to read it. If that was indeed the expectation, were my Black classmates faced with deciding if, how and when they wanted to attempt to blend in? And what might be the ramifications, academically and otherwise, if they chose to challenge the white status quo? Only time would tell.

The fall of 1966 was filled with "firsts" for many of us as we set sail on our junior high school voyage. For one, my new classmates, Dwain and Kelvin, far outnumbered by their white peers at Bruce Elementary in third through sixth grades, were thrilled to once again share classrooms with Black girls. To grasp the enormity of the situation, one only has to imagine scores of white kids, voluntarily or not, expected to adapt and adjust to minority status in a majority-Black environment of students, teachers and culture.

Reasons a'plenty why that wasn't gonna happen.

Color My World

The experience of being "other" can be fairly commonplace for people of color. Most of us white folk have never been the lone Caucasian in a conference room, swimming pool or department store; at a bar, in a classroom or at a party. Accustomed to, comfortable with and smug in our majority status, we assume that the space we inhabit and how we occupy and define it is the norm. Even if unaware of doing so, we expect others to adapt, to figure out how to conform to our circumscribed world.

One evening several years ago, a Laramie acquaintance found himself, literally, the only white person on Memphis' iconic Beale Street. That not-altogether comfortable moment showed him how being the sole minority in any given situation can feel. It is a memorable experience.

Since junior high school, I have often found myself the lone white person in gatherings, be they funerals, church services or birthday parties. My presence in those circumstances is by invitation and by choice, but being the only white person in a room is not always a comfortable experience. Imagine finding oneself in that position on a regular basis.

Jacqueline Partee

Central High School
Class of 1972

A proud graduate of a small, all-black neighborhood elementary school, I enjoyed the favor of all my teachers. I can still close my eyes and see the hallways and classrooms and smell the freshly waxed floors. I can hear my teachers' voices and feel the love and care of the principal, staff and faculty.

Attending Bellevue was a bit of a shock, though I was not alone, as one of my elementary school friends transferred with me. Along the way I met and befriended many, some of whom I remain in contact with.

As a Bellevue Junior High student, I remember feeling apprehensive and enthusiastic. Wide-eyed and afraid. Focused and awe-struck. Naive. All of this on my first day, surrounded by new faces of all shapes, colors and sizes. I don't remember all the names of those faces, but certain teachers and events do stand out in my mind.

Unfortunately, I don't recall the name of my Tennessee history teacher who took a group of us on an outing, a day that included lunch at Shoney's. When we returned to school, classes had been dismissed due to unrest in the city. Everyone left for home but me, including my neighborhood friend who had found a ride. While most students lived north, south or east of the school, I lived west of Bellevue, near downtown. City bus service to my neighborhood had been canceled, as it was closer to the outbursts and demonstrations. Scared and confused, I had no way to contact my mother. That same history teacher cared enough to drive me home, putting herself in the middle of a potentially violent situation. I'll never forget her kindness and her courage.

Author's note: The unrest Jackie refers to was in response to the assassination of Dr. King that day.

Mr. Toney, the Black band instructor, was also my geography teacher. His appreciation of my conscientious work will always have a place in my heart. I still have my assignment, "Cuba", complete with Mr. Toney's comment and grade:

"Beautiful and neat. Very well organized. Thank you. Grade: 100++."

Of course, not all the teachers at Bellevue cared. Some just marked their days. I'll never forget my first day in language arts class when I was asked to read aloud. Standing with all eyes on me, I began to read, mispronouncing the word "genuine." Oh my god! Promptly corrected, I felt so small and dumb. From that day forward I vowed to never give another teacher at Bellevue reason to correct me in such a demeaning way.

I thought about all my elementary school teachers and the work they did every day to provide a quality education for us when no one else cared. My goal from then on was to work hard and excel academically, to never again allow anyone to see me as one unworthy of respect and acknowledgment.

I Walk the Line

Bellevue Junior High boasted some quirky and outmoded policies, rules and restrictions that felt ridiculous to its incoming students in 1966. The words "GIRLS" and "BOYS" remain carved in granite lintels over entrances at some Midtown Memphis schools. They meant exactly what they said. Though our classrooms and hallways weren't divided by gender, girls and boys had to use strictly monitored separate school entrances and staircases inside the building. The cafeteria was similarly bifurcated.

And then there was Miss Marie Pansy, the girls' gym and health teacher who tolerated no nonsense, took herself very seriously and expected no less of her girls. Not one to joke around, she rarely allowed a smile to cross her face. Miss Pansy was an institution within an institution, along with several other teachers who looked like grandmothers. My perspective was, of course, skewed by the fact that my young parents were only thirty-three at the time.

Girls' entrance, Bellevue   Boys' entrance, Bellevue

Little White Lies

Miss Pansy,

You and I have not seen eye to eye on much of anything since I came to Bellevue last year. I find you completely ill-suited for your roles as girls' health and gym teacher and advisor to the cheerleaders. I don't know your age, but I know you're too old and out of touch. What we need is a fit, energetic role model, someone who can run the floor with us, someone who can shoot a basketball or do a situp. Someone who can do more than scowl and blow a whistle. Your lessons in health class are completely disconnected from where we are as young teenage girls, offering no useful information as we watch our bodies change.

Yesterday was one of the worst days of my life when, dressed in gym whites, I started my period for the first time. Completely humiliated, I had to turn to you for supplies and permission to shed my stained uniform. No one, especially me, wanted to be ushered into that phase of womanhood by you, though I'm sure I wasn't the first or last girl to find herself in that position. How embarrassing.

Your classrooms now include Black girls, a fact that seems to elude you when you warn us that "Colored" boys will look up our skirts when we're on the school stairways. Not boys in general. "Colored" boys. You obviously don't care about how your words impact your students. Day after day, we're trapped in your web of ignorance and racism and there's not a damned thing we can do about it.

As a cheerleader, I get nothing from you as an advisor except stringent and outdated regulations. Being a cheerleader should be fun but you run the program more like a regime, monitoring our routines like a hawk. You even make us kneel on the floor to ensure that our skirt hems touch the hardwood.

You have actually stated that "Colored" girls are athletically uncoordinated. Your bizarre and baseless views dominate the yearly judging process for cheerleaders. Year after year you use your influence to ensure an all-white squad. It may not happen while I'm still at Bellevue, but believe me, change will come to these hallowed halls. If you're still teaching here, I can only surmise that you will not be prepared or pleased.

I don't think for a minute that this letter would give you pause or make you reconsider your thinking. Writing it makes me feel better. If only I had the nerve to say all of this to your face, to accept an inevitable suspension. Instead, I write a letter that you'll never read.

SEM

Jive Talkin'

Friendships at Bellevue formed, for the most part, around common interests like sports, band, chorus and school clubs. Black and white kids cautiously tested the waters of interaction, quiet curiosities and thinly veiled tensions from both groups pulsing just below the surface. As with most student bodies, fights weren't unheard of and the new racial component at Bellevue increased the usual number of stand offs. Rumbles, fistfights and wrestling matches played out in the courtyard at the final bell, following dares and accusations exchanged inside the school building. Boys fought boys and girls fought girls, often with an enthusiastic audience, until a teacher ultimately broke up the fight and dispersed the crowd.

The vast majority of friendships that did develop between Black and white kids began and ended within the halls and on the playing fields of the school grounds – with the exception of a few Black and white athletes who occasionally hung out together after school. We were managing ourselves as a desegregated body, but there was little actual integration taking place as we took comfort in the safe harbor of our cliques and returned to our own worlds at the end of each school day. The very idea of breaching those racial boundaries on a broader social basis didn't enter most students' minds. Messing around with new friends at school within the parameters of sports or chorus was one thing. Inviting those friend-ships into the personal confines of home, family and neighborhood, quite another.

Ultimately, very few of us Black and white students at Bellevue walked through each others' doors, shared meals or slept in each others' homes. We seldom met each others' parents or siblings. Nor did we see movies together or swim in the same pool. There was no opportunity to dance with each other. The very concept of dating someone of another race was inconceivable. That particular line, though invisible, went unchallenged and remained, for almost everyone, a sacrosanct and venerated dictum of social norms in Memphis and throughout the South for years to come.

There was little intersection of Black and white lives in 1960s Memphis. For many of my Black friends, our family represented their entire personal relationship with the white world. I've been told by several of my former Black classmates that, to this day, more than fifty years later, I remain the only white person to have crossed the threshold of their homes. Ever. Today, segregation continues to significantly define personal lives and entire communities in Memphis.

Bridge Over Troubled Water

Eighth grade for me spanned the calendar years of 1967 and 1968.

Talk among students and conversations I overheard between my parents and their friends made it clear to me that the push for civil rights was gaining momentum across the South as Black communities grew ever more focused and cohesive. Civic leaders, pastors, educators and community groups organized and strategized. Virtually every aspect of American life, including housing, education, representation and compensation was being examined and targeted by Black leaders and a small but committed band of progressive white folks.

Little did anyone know that we Memphians, along with the rest of the world, were on the cusp of witnessing one of the most tragic events in American history.

Mississippi River bridge

CHAPTER FOUR

To Sir With Love

In 1967, Hollywood released two groundbreaking movies, both starring Sidney Poitier:

To Sir with Love and *Guess Who's Coming to Dinner* brought interracial crushes and relationships to the big screen, exploding conventional mores of the film industry.

Nineteen sixty-seven also brought sweeping, monumental changes to my personal life, a critical turning point that I could never have imagined. My life changed forever when that cinematic representation of Black and white romance came true for me. That fall, a friendship deepened between me and a Black student, son of a local pastor and civil rights leader. In the hallway one afternoon, after the final bell, Dwain handed me a folded note.

Son of a Preacher Man

Shelley,

I know this note may surprise you and I'm prepared for you to reject it out of hand. I'd like you, though, to hear me out, to at least consider what I'm asking.

I think you know that I really like you and I'm pretty sure the feelings are mutual. Otherwise, I probably wouldn't be writing this.

I'm asking you to be my girlfriend. Would you consider going with me?

There, I've said it. I know how crazy this may sound. Black boys don't date white girls.

Please think about it. If you need to say no, I'll absolutely respect your decision, but I really hope your answer is yes. I'll call you tonight.

Your friend always,

Dwain

I Second That Emotion

Dwain,

I'm so thankful that this message, meant for my eyes only, wasn't intercepted by a teacher. You were wise to give it to me after school.

Your note stopped me in my tracks when I read it on my walk home today. Until now, I hadn't allowed myself to even dream that our flirting would turn into something more, even though our mutual admiration is pretty obvious.

I guess I'm surprised that you are willing to risk so much to date me. I haven't had much experience with dating, but I'd be honored to go out with you.

I read your words to my mom right away when I got home. I'm pretty sure that nothing had prepared her for this moment. One doesn't have to look far and wide to understand that Black and white students don't date each other. Maybe up North, on the West Coast or in movies, but not in Memphis, Tennessee! Though she knows full well that her daughter is going to follow her heart, her concern lies in what others might say or do in reaction to seeing us together.

I'm sure she'll tell my dad tonight. I wonder if you've told your parents. We should probably be prepared for mixed reactions from our families and friends. So many questions. I can't wait to talk to you tonight. Thank you for this.

SEM

Everybody's Talkin'

I don't know when Dwain informed his parents of his decision to date a white girl, but there was no way that this relationship would go unnoticed. By anyone.

When we saw each other at school the next day, we knew that everything going forward in our lives would be different. Between us, there were sideways glances and knowing smiles. We were simply smitten. Dwain and I began visiting each other's homes, setting up meet and greet moments with our parents and siblings. Over dinners, we enjoyed spirited conversation and, especially in his house, plenty of teasing and laughter.

I was convinced of our destiny when we compared notes about our elementary school experiences. We discovered that we had each won spelling bees as fifth graders. That bit of serendipity was confirmed when I dug out my Commercial Appeal article, complete with headshots of the winners. Unbeknownst to us at the time, we had shared the stage during the county-wide spelling bee. He surely fared better than I in that contest.

During rehearsals at Bellevue for the school production of *So This is Paris*, we ducked behind stage curtains and slipped away to third floor recesses to steal kisses. What a thrilling time for two young people who had inexplicably chosen each other against all odds. In our bubble, we were simply two teenagers who liked each other – but we knew that we were destined to become a public curiosity. Even though we kept our relationship on the down-low as much as possible, containing our excitement wasn't easy. Too young to drive and too smart to flaunt, we spent our time together outside of school in each other's and friends' homes. On weekend nights, we went to parties. A lot of parties. With lights down as low as host parents would allow, we and our friends danced to a revolving selection of Motown, Atlantic and Stax 45s.

Whenever possible, I attended Dwain's church where his dad was pastor. How Reverend Kyles could preach and sing! I'm not sure I can explain how it felt to be a thirteen-year-old white girl in a rousing Black church service in 1967 Memphis. What I knew for sure, what fueled my audaciousness, was the simple fact that I really liked the preacher's son – and his beautiful voice. Among so many memories of those Sunday mornings, I particularly recall the day that Dwain sang a solo about a boy's love for his mother. His own mom, Gwen, was a stunning and radiant "first lady" of the church and proud mother of four. You can be sure that there was not a dry eye in that sanctuary when the last line was sung and the organ struck its final note.

The ways that Dwain and I found ourselves immersed in and engaged with each other's families and communities was completely uncharted territory for everyone involved.

In early spring of 1968, as members of the National Honor Society, he and I, along with our fellow inductees, attended an annual picnic at Overton Park. When a game of "chicken" began, I jumped on his back, eager to challenge our competitors. In response to that simple act, an undeniable chill settled over the park. Even through the resounding silence, we could sense the reactions:

"The audacity!" "How dare you!"

Kids and teachers alike couldn't believe what they were seeing.

The danger we could face for a physical display of friendship wasn't on our minds that spring day although Dwain knew better than I how imprudent it was for a young Black man to show any interest whatsoever in a young white woman. The wheels of dissent indeed began to turn, gossip swirled and the inevitable fallout from our decision to date each other started to become very real. It was impossible for us to ignore the growing strains of disapproval.

I was effectively and immediately ditched by my closest white girlfriends. Almost overnight, I became a pariah. They, and probably I, simply did not know how to bridge the new gulf that suddenly separated us, an expanse too unfamiliar to set across. Quite literally, none of us had ever come face-to-face with this particular social construct. I tried to salvage some of those connections but my white friends apparently couldn't abide my decision.

And as if that wasn't hard enough, I also faced ostracism from some Black students who, for various reasons, resented my perceived infringement on their community. I was accused of being "fast" and "easy." Why else would a white girl date a Black guy, and conversely, what other reason would a Black guy have for dating a white girl? Dwain, too, faced some initial criticism. Comments from his close friends went something like this:

"Aw man, you're running for student council president. If you have to date a white girl, at least choose someone better looking who might actually help you get elected!" My status as girlfriend obviously didn't hurt his campaign, as soon thereafter Dwain became Bellevue's first Black council president.

It didn't take long for the two of us to identify kids and families who were cool with our decision, people whose support proved critical to our young and daring relationship. With so little historical or logical reason for Black kids and their families to trust white folks, I was nevertheless welcomed into homes and lives. The fact that most of my white community could not respond in kind was painful and perplexing to me. Except for family life, my social world soon became immersed in the Black community. And there it would stay for years to come. My new friends and their families had extended a welcome that gave me a renewed sense of belonging. Important stuff for a young teenager.

I was called out of class on more than one occasion by a teacher, who, in hushed voice, asked me:

"Are your parents aware of what you're doing?"

How could they possibly have thought that I was dating a Black student without my parents' knowledge and support? No secrets here! Those teachers would have been shocked to learn how welcome Dwain and I were in each other's homes.

The Memphis city school system was still a relatively small universe at that time and news traveled quickly between schools. The fact that we were an item was soon very public knowledge, not only at Bellevue but also throughout the school district. We knew this because folk talked – everyone from kids and parents to faculty and administrators. It's pretty safe to say that out of some 130,000 students citywide, we were the only interracial junior high or high school twosome. Kids loved to gossip and rumors traveled at the speed of light. We surely would have heard of others and it would have been nice to know that we weren't alone. This assertion may be inconceivable today, as our world has grown so accustomed to friendships, partnerships, marriages and families that represent every possible combination of race and ethnicity, but ours was the sad and literal truth in 1967 Memphis.

What a terribly disconcerting time that must have been for our parents. None of us had any way of anticipating or predicting what might happen or who might initiate an unthinkable response to seeing us together. Reverend and Mrs. Kyles feared that they might look outside to find their son hanging from a street lamp. What a base, visceral dread for any parent to carry.

In looking back at what appeared to be our devil-may-care attitude when we sometimes walked to my house after school, my friend Kelvin said to me recently, "What were we thinking?" Well, quite honestly, we weren't. We were young, buoyed by naivete, audacity and foolishness. The difference, and we knew it, was that there were inquisitive eyes and dark clouds casting a pall over us wherever we went. Yet, like most teens who believe they are impervious to danger, we couldn't begin to imagine the very real threats that lurked or a vulnerability that went far beyond rude stares and denigrating verbiage. From our limited youthful perspective, bad things only happened out there somewhere, to other people. Or on the big screen. But, this wasn't Hollywood and it wasn't make-believe.

Although they were supportive of the decision we'd made, his parents and mine shared profound concerns about our safety, encouraging us at all times to make smart choices and to be attentive as we gathered. In those days, there were no cell phones for quick calls or apps with which to follow us through the city. Our folks had to trust that we would make good choices, that we would be left alone and pray that we would always make it home. Safely.

Kelvin Willis
Bellevue Junior High
Class of 1969

Bellevue Junior High, one of the "feeder" schools for Central High, was in turn "fed" by three elementary schools – Bruce, Idlewild and Rozelle. The students who came to Bellevue in the 1960s were an interesting cross section of Memphis. Idlewild had middle- to upper-class kids who came from what is now known as Central Gardens. Rozelle was much more blue collar and racially diverse. Bruce had a smattering of everything from children of professionals to lower-class white kids who lived in Lamar Terrace. There was also an infusion of Black kids from outside the district. Bellevue was quite cosmopolitan and diverse for its time. Then there was "us." Dwain Kyles and me. We spent four long years being the token Black kids in our class at Bruce.

Two things immediately caught my attention when I arrived at Bellevue. One, passing classes was fun, as we got to intermingle in the halls with our classmates. And two, four years had passed since I had been in class with a Black female. When I was placed in home room 7-4 and saw someone who was actually darker than me and a whole lot prettier, I thought I had died and gone to heaven!

For only the second time and ironically the last, Dwain and I were placed in the same home room at Bellevue. Other than fifth grade, the theory had seemingly been to divide and hopefully conquer us by putting us in separate classrooms. Mrs. Lawrence's 7-4 homeroom supposedly represented the creme de la creme of students from the feeder schools. Only three of "us" were in the home room – Dwain, the good-looking Black girl and myself.

Our first report cards of the year showed that no one in the vaunted 7-4 had made the Honor Roll. I had mostly made Bs along with a couple of As and Cs. Mrs. Lawrence tore into us: if Jaqueline Partee could do it, why couldn't we? "Who is Jacqueline Partee?" I asked. The Black girl in my class replied,

"You know, the bright-skinned girl with pretty hair who carries a briefcase!" That ended up being a life-altering moment, one that would blossom from puppy love to first love to lifelong admiration.

Bellevue was a school steeped in tradition. Being a seventh grader meant that we were at the bottom of the food chain. Separate entrances for boys and girls prevented courting before school. Bellevue colors were blue and orange and our school fight song echoed that of Notre Dame. But the craziest tradition was our mascot: the JERSEYS. On every opponent's field or court, we were heckled as the Jersey Cows and taunted with "moos." Very disconcerting to an impressionable thirteen-year-old.

The Idlewild Elementary contingent was nice enough. Ken, Jimmy, Billy, Wendell, Robin, Cathy and Shelley, to name a few. However, they had not been exposed to many Black classmates, especially those like Dwain and myself who shared their socio-economic background.

Eighth grade was different. I had made second chair, first trumpet, Jackie Partee was my first girlfriend, and I had become a leader of Bellevue's Black students. Never studious but always smart, I was inducted into the National Honor Society. As one of Bellevue's most popular students, Dwain was nominated to run for Student Council President in the spring of 1968. As his self-appointed campaign manager, I was surprised by the amount of support he was receiving. At the time, Bellevue was about thirty-five percent Black. We would need every one of those votes and some white ones to win.

Ol' Dan Cupid shot one of his arrows, hitting both Dwain and Shelley! I didn't realize it until well after the campaign was underway. Imagining my best friend's aspirations going up in smoke, my only comment to him was, "Keep this under wraps till after the election!" They did, and Dwain became Bellevue's first Black student council president.

1967-1968. What a school year! City-wide elections followed close behind the selection of Bellevue's new student government officers. My uncle, A.W. Willis, the first Black legislator in Tennessee since Reconstruction, lost his bid for mayor of Memphis in 1967. Despite that loss, A.W. remained a force in Memphis politics and law, as well as my role model and inspiration.

The fathers of two Bellevue classmates joined the city administration in 1968. Shelley's dad, Jerrold, was appointed Mayor Henry Loeb's Chief Administrative Officer. Cathy Chandler's dad, Wyeth, was elected to serve on the Memphis City Council. He went on to become mayor in 1972.

In the tumultuous spring of 1968, we eighth graders at Bellevue would have a ringside seat at an event that would forever change our world.

CHAPTER FIVE

We Are Family

To my girlfriends,

Faye, Denise, Lora, Yvonne, Connie, Anita, Deborah, Jackie - you all know who you are.

For reasons that I can't totally comprehend, you have welcomed this pale girl into your circle. I have had the pleasure of meeting your families and on occasion, sharing meals and joining slumber parties in your homes. In our world, this is unprecedented. I am your first white friend and you are my first Black girl friends. A door was opened wide for us all when Dwain and I began dating. You didn't have to invite me in, but you did.

At the risk of admitting gross and inexcusable ignorance, I'm only now aware of the nuances of Black culture in your homes that I previously never had reason to consider. It's becoming clear to me that, in critically important ways, you all and I do not see the world through the same lens or the same looking glass.

I look at magazine covers and models, mannequins and actors, cartoon and book characters and I see myself, my world. All white. Except for the Jet and Ebony issues that you've introduced me to - who knew? - and the rare sighting of a Black actor on TV or a movie screen, you see someone else's world. All white. So few literary or commercial images that you can relate to or connect with, so few that reflect who you are. Black girls. Strong, beautiful, important and smart, capable of anything you set your minds to.

When we get together, what we have in common is clear, but we're discovering ways in which life in our homes, neighborhoods and churches looks, sounds and feels so very different. The paintings and photographs on your walls depict Black life. It never occurred to me that, of course, the art and photography in your homes would reflect your families and communities. It never occurred to me because I had no frame of reference. Now I do.

I marvel at the carefully curated trifecta of saviors that grace many of your living room walls: Jesus, John F. Kennedy and Martin Luther King, Jr. The seating in those rooms, often protected by clear plastic covering, is reserved for guests and special occasions. Conversely, our living room is a mashup of bohemian and contemporary design and furnishing and is, more often than not, filled with lounging teenagers.

We laugh until we cry as we attempt to parse out some of the intricacies and intimacies of our lives:

You: "Why do you shave your legs?"
Me: "Why don't you?

You: "Why do you curl your hair?"
Me: "Why do you straighten yours?"

And on and on. We curiously compare the textures of our hair and various styling techniques. We discuss our favorite foods, books and dance moves and share family nicknames. We're learning that our cultures, traditions, family histories and lore can, and often do, look distinctly different. It feels to me like we're in separate boats on the same ocean - if that is indeed the case, I'm just happy that we share these waters.

Discussions and interactions in my household tend toward the serious. The banter, humor and expressions of affection I experience in your homes aren't familiar to me. I love listening to those good-natured familial exchanges, even though I'm sometimes the intended target of a joke.

When I'm dropped off to join you at a party in Orange Mound or over on Parkway, my light skin, hair and blue eyes draw plenty of attention. Those moments make me even more acutely aware of what you all encounter within the walls of our school. At our ages, being "other," regardless of circumstance, is not a particularly comfortable or preferred status.

In the notebooks that quietly circulate among us, someone has assigned me the moniker of "BESS." Blue-eyed soul sister. While I love and appreciate the gesture, I'll surely be "outed" immediately by any teacher lucky enough to get his or her hands on such a journal. Those notebooks, our early forms of social media, are filled with gossip, which can be cruel or kind. There's not much middle ground as we dis or compliment, announce crushes or rejections and unleash jealousies and rumors.

I'm reminded of the old song *Polka Dots and Moonbeams* when you all tease Dwain and me about what our children might look like: striped, dotted, half and half? Oh, please! At age thirteen, babies are hardly on our radar, but I get it. That's where thoughts go when "mixed" couples are part of the equation.

In your moms', aunties' and grandmas' kitchens, I am welcomed by warm greetings and mouth-watering aromas: pots of greens and black-eyed peas, always seasoned with ham hocks. Cornbread, tender pot roasts and sinfully delicious desserts, still warm from the oven, sit on countertops.

Occasionally, I'm left queasy by mingling smells of stewing chitlins and hot irons being pulled through hair. The irony isn't lost on me that I torture myself with oversized plastic curlers every night in order to achieve the opposite effect. With all due respect, I have to leave the chitlins alone.

Whether or not we know it, as we ride city buses together, window shop downtown or wander the sidewalks of each others' neighborhoods, we are representing the shakers and movers of our generation. It's clear that our communities and the people of Memphis in general are not quite ready for the likes of us. Sometimes we get a little rowdy, but even in quiet ways, we are girls leading the charge,

consciously, deliberately and courageously. I feel
certain that as we age and renew our connections
we'll look back on these days with wonder, pride
and deep affection.

SEM

Girls Just Want To Have Fun

For an active kid like me, the fact that girls weren't offered organized
school sports was a travesty. Lacking any option to play competitive
basketball, softball, field hockey or volleyball, in eighth grade I decided
to try cheerleading. A month of practicing for tryouts left my legs crying
out in pain, buckling at the sight of stairs. Following in my sister's
footsteps and despite the fact that I could barely walk, I was chosen
for the squad. In ninth grade, I was reelected and again we performed
the same array of stiff and calculated routines in our blue and orange
uniforms. No unladylike splits, flips or cartwheels for us.

Having watched the soulful cheers of several squads from competing
Black schools, I suggested that we consider changing up our program.
Those girls were cool in their cute short skirts and easy moves. We most
certainly were not. I decisively lost that fight when my fellow cheerleaders,
all white, begged to differ.

Later that year, my circle of Black girlfriends and I had grown increasingly
frustrated that they were passed over every year in cheerleading tryouts.
This, despite the fact that the success of our boys' basketball, baseball
and football teams depended on the skills of a number of Black student
athletes. We petitioned, we argued and we reasoned but the judges
refused to select even one Black girl from the candidates. When yet
another round of tryouts for ninth grade produced an all-white squad,

my friends and I decided to stage a protest at the end of a pep rally. You might imagine, correctly, that this didn't end well for me.

Big Girls Don't Cry

Mr. Gilbert,

Well, that was quite a session. I suppose, in retrospect, I should be thankful for not being subjected to a paddling. As an office aide, I'm accustomed to hearing the wailing of offenders as you smack them across the buttocks and legs. Your instrument of punishment is a wooden paddle crafted in shop class, complete with holes for maximum effect. Between classes, white teachers and coaches wield the paddles, intimidating and threatening boys in the hallways, baiting them for even a suggestion of insubordination or disrespect. They seem to find special pleasure in targeting Black students. That's profiling and harassment. I know, I get it. You all want to teach "them" a thing or two. I wonder what lessons "they" learn from your beatings. What you are practicing, sir, is nothing less than corporal punishment.

I was singled out after a brief protest that my Black girlfriends and I started at the end of today's pep rally. We have repeatedly petitioned the school for equal representation on the cheerleading squad, to reflect the diversity in our school and on the boys' sports teams. And yet, another round of cheerleader tryouts has ended with an all-white selection. Yes,

I was involved in planning today's protest. The rest of the unsuspecting cheerleaders left the auditorium stage while I stayed behind, joining my friends in a rousing cheer. It was really a pretty benign attempt to make our point, to simply be heard.

Our protest ended promptly when the bell rang and everyone but me returned to class. As I sat opposite you at your desk, you berated and chastised me for what you consider errant and disruptive behavior. You even called my mom in, probably assuming that you and she would be in agreement. You were wrong. I joined Mr. Robinson's algebra class, already in session, with telltale red eyes, having learned nothing from my encounter with you. You don't know how to effectively listen to or communicate with your students. It feels like we're not supposed to have opinions or voices.

As the adult in the room, your only instinct seems to be punishment and humiliation. I know you think I'm nothing but a troublemaker, a white girl who inexplicably dares to cross and challenge established racial lines. I admit that I can be defiant with a healthy dose of attitude. But the concerns we're raising and the requests we're making are important and relevant. It'd be best to take us seriously, to be proactive rather than reactive. The new face of our school is here to stay. Bellevue will never return to a predominantly white campus. This diverse student body offers new dimensions and raises an abundance of issues never before dealt with in the Memphis public school system.

I'll not apologize for what I did today and I can't promise to "behave" myself going forward. I am sorry that we cannot seem to find our way to productive dialogue. Our school needs and deserves an honest look at where we are and at what needs to be considered as we move ahead. Without that commitment, all of our experiences at Bellevue will be clouded with resentment and distrust.

SEM

CHAPTER SIX

The Sounds Of Silence

In Memphis, my parents joined Central Christian Church, located across the street from the new main public library at Peabody and McLean, within a few blocks of Idlewild Elementary. Our little world in the big city was extremely compact and convenient.

The five of us became active members of the church, attending services or programs twice on Sunday and Wednesday night. Sonya, Lissa and I eventually joined the choir, which practiced on yet another weeknight. Bob and Jerry served as reluctant recruits when extra male voices were needed. We were all in.

When the organ struck the familiar notes, I sang my heart out to standards like *The Old Rugged Cross*, *In the Garden* and our minister's favorite, *Blessed Assurance*. The fact that I, a girl who didn't love an audience, was selected to sing solos speaks volumes to the lack of vocal depth and talent in our choir. In consecutive years, I was assigned *O Holy Night* and *Lo How a Rose E'er Blooming*, neither of which is particularly easy for even a trained voice to perform. From where I stand today, it's inconceivable to me that I stood alone at the dais and got through those pieces.

As junior high students, my Black friends and I sometimes attended each others' churches. I was always welcomed by their congregations, but the folks at my church weren't terribly excited about seeing Black visitors walk through the door. I began to learn the hard lesson that not even the pledges of Christianity could ease or honestly address the persistent sting of racism and segregation.

Despite the cold, wet weather that often greeted Memphians on Easter Sunday, women and girls shivered their way through the day, determined to show off competing finery. Each year, Lissa and I looked forward to new dresses, sewn by our mom until we mastered the art well enough to make our own.

Lissa and Shelley, Atlanta Easter, 1957

A lot of planning and preparation went into the holiday, the whole of Easter being nothing less than a full scale production: the planning and execution of outfits; a proliferation of potted lilies in church; seasonal choral selections; an agonizingly long sermon; a children's musical extolling frilly bonnets and parades; and last but by no means least, the traditional ham and scalloped potato dinner awaiting us at home.

That celebratory morning in 1969 became a benchmark moment – one that ended up affecting many lives – when the associate minister welcomed into our service a Black family whose car had broken down enroute to their own church. He ushered them to seats through the main door at the back of the sanctuary, so discreetly that most of us were unaware of their presence during the service. Someone obviously noticed and the response was swift. For his act of kindness and inclusion, that minister was fired. Christianity at its finest, with a terrible outcome.

My parents were shocked and angry, knowing full well that their questions and protestations would be met by a deafening silence. For years, our church had allowed cruel rumors to circulate amongst its membership and had looked the other way when extramarital affairs became impossible to ignore. Those gross examples of hypocrisy, coupled with this latest scandal, drove my parents from the church and away from organized religion. We kids were given full rein to form our own conclusions, to make our own decisions. By year's end, all five of us had left that church. I was fourteen.

Aquarius – Let The Sun Shine

In 1967, prior to the upheaval in our church, Sonya and Jerry joined an ecumenical group in establishing the Half and Half Coffee House on Cleveland Street in Midtown. No one living can recall the meaning behind its name. The new endeavor was a natural extension of my parents' role as church youth-group leaders. Located only a few blocks from our house on Vance, the Half and Half became our home away from home on many a Friday and Saturday night.

The mission of the coffee house was to provide a supportive gathering place for teenagers and young adults. Mirroring the look of big-city coffee houses with its lowlights and casual atmosphere, the Half and Half provided the perfect backdrop for performances by poets and musicians. It was an oasis, a sanctuary of sorts, offering young people a safe place to voice their questions, concerns and confusions. The welcoming environment provided an opening for conversations that weren't shared by most families at a time when a grim, quiet determination to tough it out often overrode opportunities for deeper connection.

As they awaited their draw in the draft lottery, young men contemplated the wisdom of engaging in the Vietnam conflict. Young women considered new and exciting options for themselves, even as they worried about the futures of brothers and boyfriends. Previously accepted mores of society and the political realm were no longer automatically endorsed, accepted or embraced. It seemed like everything was up for debate, including organized religion, race relations and sexual identity. Elements of the youth culture exploded; long hair and afros accompanied bell bottoms and dashikis. The voices and messages of folk, rock and roll and soul musicians captured the attention of young people, as impassioned lyrics by troubadour Bob Dylan and others heralded that the times were indeed a'changing.

In many ways, I came of age in that electric environment. I watched as my parents' involvement in the Half and Half signaled a turning point in their personal lives, when they found that like-minded community. Ironically, given their eventual departure from the church, almost all of my folks' closest friends remained practicing clergy and their families. That small alliance of committed and engaged progressives coalesced into a supportive network that would prove critically important when April of 1968 rolled around.

Sonya Moore
Author's mother

Sonya, Laramie, 2014

Since our move to Memphis in 1962, my time had been taken up with three children and commitments at Central Christian Church, where Jerry and I sponsored the teen youth group and where I sang in the choir. By 1967, the kids were in junior high school and their lives were expanding with friends and activities. As Director of the City Planning Commission, Jerry worked long hours. I was ready for more community involvement, but could never have anticipated what lay ahead. Our good friend, Dix Archer, who had his thumb on the pulse of progressive Memphis, gave me names, numbers and encouragement.

Myra Dreifus was one such contact. She directed a group of women who worked on behalf of underserved children in select Black elementary schools. With a focus first on nutrition, the Fund for Needy School Children persuaded the school district to simply provide a carton of milk for kids who came to school hungry. That project grew into today's National School Lunch program. I've since learned that dairy products are difficult to digest by many Black people. So much for good intentions. Women with the Fund also worked with students who needed directed attention, providing badly needed assistance to classroom teachers.

I signed up to work at Hyde Park Elementary in North Memphis. One call to the principal, Mr. Bland, and I was on my way. With absolutely no idea what I was doing on my first day and a sinking feeling in the pit of my stomach, I quietly observed a white teacher and her fifteen Black first graders.

One student in particular concerned the teacher. Ricky missed too many days of school and his excuse was consistent: "My uncle wears the clothes on those days." I was asked to visit Ricky's mom, Mary. I don't recall how she was informed of my impending arrival, but when Mary opened her front door, she and I both took for granted that I had a right to be there. We also must have known that our roles would never be reversed.

Mary led me through her front room, which held a small television and furniture covered in clear plastic. She showed me her bedroom and a larger one dedicated to her nine children, ranging in age from three to fifteen. That room held makeshift beds and little spare floor space. Not a toy or book in sight. A table without chairs sat in her kitchen, the cupboard was almost bare and there was no sign of recent cooking. Her tiny bathroom was filthy. Throughout most of the house were massive piles of ragged, dirty clothes. Signs of roaches and mice were everywhere. The poverty evident in Mary's house was something I'd never encountered. There was nothing to compliment and I dared not comment or judge.

After taking several loads of clothes home with me to launder, a friend and I procured and installed a wringer washer in Mary's kitchen. At least she would have the option of doing her family's laundry.

When I learned that Mary had been admitted to a hospital psychiatric ward, I checked on her kids. The younger ones had been farmed out to her mother and the older ones were left to fend for themselves. I used Mary's meager monthly assistance funds to buy groceries for the kids left at home.

I was asked to take Ricky to the University of Tennessee teaching hospital for evaluation of chronic stomach pain. Imagine my surprise when the attending doctor turned out to be my neighbor, Pat Wall. Without the benefit of overnight observation, Dr. Wall was unable to diagnose or treat Ricky's symptoms. We retraced the yellow footprints that led us out of the building, back to our respective worlds.

As often as I saw Mary that year, I didn't feel that my efforts would significantly change her situation. I found myself in a position akin to delivering Thanksgiving baskets to those "in need" – a nice gesture that served no enduring purpose or solved any underlying issue. Consciousness of the deep crosscurrents I experienced while working with Mary and her family are only now surfacing fifty years later. My part of that equation was privilege, a realization that continues to shame and haunt me.

The coffee house trend hit Memphis in 1967 when clergy and congregants of three Midtown churches began to explore ways of attracting greater numbers of teenagers to their membership rolls. It was decided that a coffee house format might accomplish that objective. I signed on as soon as I heard about the proposal. In early 1968 our group met to discuss plans for a space that would bring together a cross section of young people who simply needed a comfortable, supportive and safe place to hang out. Our future endeavor was christened the Half and Half Coffee House.

The first thing we needed was a home for our concept. A lease was soon signed on an empty storefront on Cleveland Street, just across from Central High School's Crump Stadium. The new space abutted a neighborhood bar which soon became a late-night haunt for us adults. I had spare time and ideas about how to spruce up the interior of the place. Despite the fact that our church body had declined my request to sponsor the Coffee House, several members were willing to get their hands dirty and help remove years' worth of city grime. Volunteers repaired the floor with scavenged lumber and replaced old windows. Others donated tables, chairs, a piano and serviceware for coffee and tea.

Because our target clientele was young people, relevant parameters were set: no drugs or alcohol on the premises. The doors were open eight to midnight, Fridays and Saturdays. Musicians with guitars strapped on their backs and poets with worn notebooks were among those who came to check out the new joint. Nearby neighbors soon voiced displeasure at the packed-house crowds and after only a few months, our landlord asked us to vacate the building.

The Coffee House moved to its second and final location at Union, near Cooper, and work immediately began on improving both the interior and exterior of the building. Inside, a paint party produced a black ceiling and orange-hued walls, while outside walls were painted a sunny yellow. A small room in the southwest corner, sectioned off with wire mesh and a door, became a poster and book shop, named "Signs of the Times." In addition to purchased inventory, work by local artists was sold on consignment. The little shop, open on weekday afternoons, never turned a profit but it did inspire just enough interest to keep the shelves stocked. It marked my first independent enterprise.

The Coffee House was a hive of activity. Jerry Lovett was hired as Director and served as in-house counselor to young people. Local musicians who appreciated a microphone and an attentive audience covered the folk music of Bob Dylan, Joan Baez, Simon and Garfunkel, Judy Collins, Joni Mitchell,

Donovan and many others. Regular attendees increased in number as we offered more services and entertainment. We were known to gather for glasses of wine or late-night meals of scrambled eggs after cleaning the Coffee House. For those of us who kept the place humming along, hard work and good times went hand in hand.

On the evening of April 4, 1968, Dr. King was assassinated in Memphis. The city was beset with anger, denial and fear. Tension filled our own home when a threatening phone call targeted Shelley. Jerry worked overtime and then some at City Hall in his new position as Chief Administrative Officer under Mayor Henry Loeb. Before that fateful April evening, I, along with two of my kids, Bob and Lissa, attended an event at Mason Temple. We were joined by friends, Bill and Elizabeth Aldridge. Anticipating an appearance by Dr. King, the place was packed with striking sanitation workers and a sea of supporters. Bill was one of a few white clergy who joined their Black colleagues on the stage; the rest of us found our way to the balcony after realizing that all main-floor seats had been taken. Four kind souls yielded their seats to us – for me, another memorable, uncomfortable moment cloaked in privilege. That night is engraved on my heart, when our white faces stood out in that crowd of some four thousand Black attendees. My husband worked in city administration, one of my daughters dated Black students and close family friends marched in downtown protests. What a confluence of roles and personal choices.

In the wake of Dr. King's murder, questions arose about the advisability of Fund volunteers continuing to work in Black neighborhoods. I forged ahead with my commitments, never feeling uneasy or threatened in the least. Before the school year ended, my thoughts turned to the need for a summer program for the Hyde Park kids. Superintendent of Schools, John

Freeman, approved my five-week proposal which relied on use of the school facility. Friends Carl and Robin Walters identified those who would support my endeavor, financially and otherwise. Charles Warren, a Southwestern professor, offered to coach older boys in basketball. (A teachable moment occurred when he transported an injured player to the Methodist Hospital. In that segregated facility, the Black athlete was refused treatment until Mr. Warren, a white man, agreed to pay the bill in full.)

By mid-June we were in business, weekdays nine to noon. Younger boys and girls enjoyed any competitive game involving speed and balls. My three kids contributed their time with various art projects. When I realized that three ten-year-old boys weren't participating in organized activities, I planned field trips for them. Off we went in my car, reading street signs along the way, visiting City Hall, the River Walk, the Zoo and other local sites. When the summer heat became unbearable, I took my three charges to a newly desegregated public swimming pool. After showering in their cutoffs, the boys joined me, wading into a pool filled with silent, disbelieving white people. No one hassled us, but we most certainly were not made to feel welcome. Our presence in an East Memphis pool surely made for interesting conversation around dinner tables that night.

Tactics and strategies didn't drive my decisions. My naivete was trumped by my principles. It's a wonder I didn't cause a lot of trouble for our family. I am grateful to everyone who stood behind and beside me in this experience and I often think fondly of those Hyde Park kids who welcomed me and allowed me to enter a corner of their lives.

CHAPTER SEVEN

Stormy Weather

The work of the City of Memphis sanitation workers, "garbage men," was grotesque. With no tidy, secured plastic liners back in the day, garbage cans were filled with household trash and foodstuff; flies and maggots, juices and slime were inevitable. The insufferable heat of summer months created the worst possible working conditions for sanitation crews. Because the employees weren't granted city-issued uniforms, they were forced to shed filthy clothes at the end of each work day before entering their own homes. One two-week pay stub from January 1968 shows net wages of $137.13 for ninety labor hours. There was no paid sick leave or overtime compensation. No shelter provided, no bathroom available. If rains commenced early in the day, the workers, who relied upon weekly checks to support their families, were sent home with a mere two-hours' pay on the books.

During the winter of 1968, an unspeakable tragedy occurred. In a desperate attempt to escape pounding rainstorms on a cold and wet February day, two workers, Echol Cole and Robert Walker – *say their names* – climbed into the back of their assigned truck. They were crushed to death when the vehicle's mechanical system short circuited and activated the hydraulic ram, pulling the two men into the garbage-filled cavity of the truck.

As a direct result of these catastrophic and wholly preventable deaths, and despite the fact that the city charter forbade employee strikes, several hundred beleaguered and grieving sanitation workers walked off the job. Their demands included improved working conditions, a pay increase schedule and the right to organize for benefits. This group of men who risked everything in their decision to walk off the job, was sustained by churches and community groups. Supporters raised funds to feed, provide transportation and pay rent and house notes for the workers and their families for the duration of the strike.

I Am A Man mural, commemorating 1968 sanitation strike

National union leaders from the AFSCME - American Federation of State, County and Municipal Employees - arrived to help organize the strike. Considered outsiders and grandstanders, their presence did little to ease tensions between the striking workers and the city administration. The Mayor was loath to negotiate with anyone - not clergy, not civic or union leaders.

In the meantime, household and commercial trash piled up in cans, overflowing onto curbs and sidewalks. Temporary workers, hired by the city to pick up garbage, were no match for the volumes of refuse collecting on the streets of Memphis.

Southern Man

The Mayor of Memphis in 1968 was Henry Loeb, son of an upper-class family that owned and operated a line of BBQ restaurants and dry cleaners throughout the city. A descendant of German Jews who immigrated to Memphis in the 1860s, Loeb enjoyed the privileges of a wealthy white southern family.

After boarding school, college and military service, Loeb served as Memphis Public Works Commissioner from 1956 to 1960. At that time the city was governed by a mayor and a five-member commission. As a commissioner, Loeb oversaw the city sanitation workers and like his predecessors, refused to provide uniforms or restroom facilities. Grievance procedures and attempts to organize were off the table.

Loeb's first term as Mayor ran from 1961 until 1963, when a family crisis prompted his early resignation. His second mayoral term began in 1967 when the commissioners were replaced with an elected city council. Loeb's final term in office ended in 1971.

After serving as Planning Director for six years, my father accepted the appointment as CAO – Chief Administrative Officer – under Mayor Loeb and was sworn into that position in January of 1968. As local newspapers confirmed, Loeb chose Jerry based on his steady manner and his impressive accomplishments as Planning Director.

A Hard Day's Night

Though they were both registered Democrats, my dad and Henry Loeb represented polar opposites of the social and political spectrum. Well aware of that dichotomy, the two men agreed to leave their differences at the door while working inside City Hall. I, and many others, have questioned how Jerry reconciled working directly under a man who was an avowed segregationist and obstructionist. Even after numerous conversations through the years with my dad on the subject, I can't offer a plausible explanation for that unlikely pairing. What does make sense to me is this: my father wasn't hired to be a Loeb loyalist. He was hired to work for the people of Memphis. Jerry had a job to do and as a dedicated public servant he made sure he did it well. It may be as simple as that.

In February of 1968, Mayor Loeb found himself underwater, consumed by the strike. Just after my dad assumed the role of CAO, Loeb directed Jerry, just shy of his thirty-fourth birthday, to take the reins of all city departments until the mayor could regain control of his city. A city that was quickly unraveling amidst the divisiveness of the labor strike.

Those months proved to be terribly exhausting and difficult for my dad, both personally and professionally. He had to remain focused on city administration and on efforts to dig Memphis out of a deep financial deficit. He also needed to pay close attention to the strike. His days at work grew longer and increasingly stressful. When he finally arrived home at night, my father didn't want to talk about much of anything, especially city government.

The Memphis City Council was reluctant to become involved in the few negotiations that did take place between the strikers, their representatives and the Mayor's office. Tensions rose within City Hall. Tempers flared. The city was on edge.

An unimaginable quantity of garbage overflowed into streets and became an overwhelming problem for every resident, neighborhood, institution and business. At that point, cool weather was the city's only saving grace.

Loeb dismissed the workers' petitions, holding fast to a court-ordered injunction prohibiting strikes by municipal employees. The sanitation workers refused to return to their jobs without at least some concessions from the city. The standoff continued with no discernable path to a settlement.

The Longest Walk

Dr. Martin Luther King, Jr. was called to Memphis in March of 1968 by local civil rights leaders and Black clergy, many of whom were one and the same. Among others, that list included the Reverends Billy Kyles, Jim Lawson and Ben Hooks.

With a clear focus on issues affecting southern states, Dr. King was, without question, the pivotal and charismatic leader of the national civil rights movement. Unmatched was his brilliance as an orator, his commitment to the uplifting of the Black community and his insistence upon social, economic and racial justice and reconciliation. Perhaps Dr. King's greatest strength was his proven willingness to walk the walk.

He and his colleagues were busy organizing a massive Poor People's March on Washington slated for later that summer. But, because the sanitation strike was seen as emblematic of so much suffering and injustice in the American Black community, Dr. King was asked to lend his name and his support to the effort. A march was planned and executed. When that event was cut short by violent confrontations between the police and marchers, a frustrated and disappointed Dr. King flew home to Atlanta.

With no new contract for the striking workers in sight and with a renewed commitment to nonviolence by local leaders, Dr. King agreed to return to Memphis on April 3. A second march was set for April 5. In rooms of the Black-owned Lorraine Motel, colleagues gathered to strategize details for the upcoming march. Everyone involved desperately needed this protest to remain peaceful and purposeful.

On the evening of April 4, 1968, Dr. King was preparing to leave the Lorraine Motel with Reverend Kyles, Andrew Young, Jesse Jackson and others for dinner in the Kyles' home. Dwain's mom and a crew of church women had spent the day cooking and baking. Men from the church had arranged tables and chairs for the anticipated meal. With places set and food prepared, the host family and church members eagerly awaited the mens' arrival. The group of men would not enter the Kyles' house until very late that night and Dr. King would not be among the guests. When friends and colleagues finally gathered to break bread, I am told that the house was filled with a quiet rage and deep sorrow.

Martin Luther King, Jr. was assassinated that evening, just after 6 p.m. on the balcony of the Lorraine Motel. For years he had lived under constant threat and in a speech to an overflow crowd at Mason Temple on the night of April 3, Dr. King implied that his days were numbered. The evening ushered in a powerful wind and rain storm that shook the windows of the Temple, an ominous night followed the next day by an unimaginable loss.

Mason Temple, Memphis, site of Dr. King's final public address

Lorraine Motel, Memphis
Wreath marks the location of Dr. King's assassination

Within minutes of the fatal shot, city officials began to place calls. Unable to reach Mayor Loeb, Fire and Police Commissioner Frank Holloman phoned Jerry. With a heavy heart, my dad took the short walk to Loeb's office. Interrupting a meeting, he informed the Mayor that Dr. King had been shot. Soon thereafter, he was pronounced dead. When other officials joined them in the Mayor's office, Jerry's eyes met those of the city's first Black council members, James Netters, Fred Davis and J.O. Patterson, Jr. Silently sharing their shock and grief, he knew that words with them would have to wait for a more private moment.

No one was allowed to drive on the curfewed streets. Sequestered in his office, Jerry called to make sure that we were all in the house, including my mom's parents who had arrived for a visit two days earlier. My small-town Wyoming grandparents couldn't have been more surprised to suddenly find themselves witness to and in the midst of a national crisis. We watched in disbelief as local and national news reports hit the homes and streets of Memphis like a lightning bolt, erupting into a firestorm of rage and fear. Rumors were impossible to contain. From any angle, every Memphis neighborhood was a powder keg of emotion and reaction. National Guard tanks and troops were deployed to enforce the sweeping curfew and to assist with garbage collection. City schools closed. Memphis went on lockdown.

With special dispensation from the city, Coretta Scott King flew to Memphis from Atlanta. On April 8, only four days after her husband was senselessly murdered, she led a march of 42,000 silent and reverent mourners; at just thirteen, I will never forget being part of that grieving mass of humanity, a collage of age, color and orientation that flowed through the downtown streets of Memphis like a river of tears.

There was no apparent resolution to the strike. With the assassination fresh in the hearts and minds of America and with riots threatening to tear cities apart, President Lyndon Johnson sent a cabinet under secretary to help negotiate a settlement between the city and the striking workers. Along with other officials, Jerry represented the city in those talks. His health suffered under the strain, as a long-time smoking habit increased to three packs a day. His suits hung on an increasingly thin frame. And still, my dad's personal response to the assassination had to take a back seat to his professional obligations. The striking men needed to return to work and Memphis needed to begin the painfully slow process of rising from the ashes. The eyes and ears of Memphians, indeed the entire nation, were keyed into this process.

When the negotiated terms, including the right to organize and the promise of a raise schedule ended the sixty-four day strike on April 16, 1968, most of the sanitation workers returned to their jobs. However, the relatively short duration of the walkout held no relationship to the gaping national wound inflicted when Dr. King was murdered. For better and worse, that labor strike and the assassination of Dr. King will undoubtedly remain *the* defining chapter in Memphis' documented history.

Robert Kennedy was assassinated a short eight weeks after Dr. King was killed. For me and probably many other young people it seemed that our country was spiraling out of control. We were too young for much critical perspective on the horrors that were unfolding, but even considering our limited capacity to process such tragedy, we could sense the gravity of the times.

Melissa Moore
Central High School
Class of 1971

Lissa, Central High Senior, 1971

I was fourteen years old on April 4, 1968; old enough to have lived through the first years of school desegregation in the South; old enough to know the shame of hypocrisy of southern churches who talked reams of "being one in God's eyes," yet who allowed Black people through their sacred doors only in the roles of janitors or maids. Old enough to feel deep in my soul that something was terribly wrong.

Recent newspaper accounts had shown a rail-thin Black man holding a placard which read: I AM A MAN. Neatly dressed in work clothes, his face revealing the tenor of his life, a black hat almost jaunty on his head, his was the countenance of one who knew justice from injustice. The story that had evoked sorrow, protest and fury was an unimaginable account of two sanitation workers, scooped up into the back of a garbage truck and crushed to death. They were simply seeking shelter from the rain.

On April 3, my dad was at his office, confined by the pressing matters of the city in a crisis not yet full blown. My mother and I were in attendance at Mason Temple, a looming gray monolith wrapped in inner-city light. Under an officially mandated curfew that we were violating, I wondered to myself whether our little yellow Volkswagen Beetle, parked in a tow-away zone in front of a dumpster, would still be there when we emerged.

We made our way through the assembly, feeling grateful to nearby strangers with weary but expectant Black faces who had offered their seats. I chose to sit with my teenage legs launched over the balcony, my neck adjusting to the impairment of the metallic guardrails. To this day, I do not know what my mother, seated just behind me, was thinking.

As the assembled "congregation" waited long minutes for the arrival of Dr. King, a spokesman asked us to reach deep into our pockets to show our support for the cause. Purses opened, pockets rustled. Instead of small collection plates, full-sized galvanized trash cans were passed along to collect the funds. By the time the cans made it to the final rows, they were filled to overflowing with cash.

With warnings of tornadoes in the area, the wind whipped and lashed heavy rain against the temple's enormous, multi-paned windows. The crowd was hushed by reverberating claps of thunder. The physicality of it is still tangible: the damp smell of two thousand overheating bodies damp from the rain, packed together in a capacity-filled space. Fanning ourselves against the humidity. Waiting. Who knew what was to come? An expectant, nearly impatient hum of as yet undisclosed history filled the building. Dr. King arrived soon thereafter.

We now know that Dr. King was begging off his appearance before the crowd. He was tired, feverish, reluctant and uninspired. He resisted. The assembled *insisted. Refusal, it seems, is not an option when one has a date with destiny. Ringed by his closest friends and advisors, he entered directly underneath the balcony and strode to the podium as the building shook.*

Dr. King spoke without apparent notes. The longer he expounded, the deeper into himself he drew. It was as if he were in dialogue with an unseen presence, not the thousands who sat before him. By the "mountaintop" portion of his speech, he was drenched in sweat. The elegance of his cadence was as sharp as a lightning bolt, the thickness of his incantation calling forth bursts of thunder.

There was little preparation in my life for the presence of the absolute power absorbed that night. Martin Luther King, Jr. was thirty-nine years old when he died the following day. My father, at thirty-four, had recently joined the city administration as Mayor Loeb's Chief Administrative Officer. As such, he represented the city in negotiations with the striking sanitation workers.

I wish I could tell you that I had had the courage of direct action. By virtue of being a member of a remarkable family, I have had examples of the personal courage required to live one's convictions. Yet, at that time in Memphis, all kinds of dreams, hopes and youthful optimism were being shattered by the truths of racism and the cruel war raging in Vietnam - as well as a creeping terror that it was not possible to live one's own life with integrity, without confrontation or threats of death. It was a time of growing up too fast. In 1968, structures that we had taken for granted were being pulled apart.

It was also a time of spiritual crisis. It seemed that as more happened externally in the country, the more I wanted to flee. Being an adolescent at such a time only compounded the confusion. When Robert Kennedy was killed on my birthday of that same year, my world crumbled. We were becoming a leaderless generation.

Teach Your Children

Dear Mrs. Hooks,

Let there be no doubt that a single adult can illuminate and influence one young person's life in immeasurable ways. Let me be that young person and you, that adult. Your love, warmth and wisdom guide and encourage me in countless ways.

Thank you for bringing together this consortium of Memphians in the wake of Dr. King's assassination. Understanding the turbulence threatening our city, you have wisely convened a racially diverse cross section of young people and adults to form a focus group. We've named our collaboration People Power Project, or PPP. When we meet on Thursdays at the Half and Half Coffee House, the only thing we know for sure is this: our school environments are in chaos and our city is broken. We need an outlet for a range of feelings and a road map to help us navigate our way through this terribly divisive and confusing time.

You have ensured that we represent a number of Memphis public schools, some only recently desegregated. Our responses to Dr. King's murder run the gamut: rage, resentment and bitterness. Shock, blame and fear. In our schools, the vast majority of Black kids and a handful of white kids are outraged and grieving. There's also a prevailing sense among Black students that all white people bear responsibility, either implicitly or explicitly, for Dr. King's murder.

I would say that most white kids in our schools are simply terrified, afraid that Black folks are plotting some kind of mass retaliation. We've even heard kids trivializing, celebrating Dr. King's death. On the evening of April 4, I received a call from a fellow white student, expressing glee about the successful "hit." Needless to say, that was an exceedingly short phone call.

Already struggling with newly desegregated student bodies, the hallways of our schools now feel like two distinct universes. No matter our personal position on recent events, all of our lives have been upended. Every adult who works with us in PPP understands that and offers his or her own critical perspective: guidance counselor, teacher, clergy, civil servant, community leader. You have introduced us to two particularly important mentors.

The Reverend James Lawson is one. He offers the critical relevance of nonviolent civil disobedience in protests. As one of several civil rights leaders who took to the airwaves to plead for calm in the wake of Dr. King's assassination, Reverend Lawson's message is exactly what we all need to hear right about now. Little did we know that Reverend Lawson would also inspire and instruct none other than the Honorable John Lewis, a tireless advocate for civil rights who served seventeen terms as a United States Representative from the great State of Georgia before his death in 2020.

Another mentor is Detective Ed Redditt, one of two Black police officers assigned to lookout posts near the Lorraine Motel on April 4. Both officers were inexplicably taken off duty just hours before Dr. King was shot. Since the assassination, conspiracy theories have circulated, centered on whether or not local, state and federal authorities were complicit in the murder. Detective Redditt doesn't dwell on questions that will likely never be answered.

You all help create an environment that makes it safe for us to argue, disagree, agree to disagree, cry, laugh and generally unload. Thursdays' sessions can get pretty real and raw as we lay it all bare. Being brutally honest in our dialogue means that feelings get hurt and best of intentions bruised. We'll come out of this stronger and closer, with a deeper understanding of where to go from here. We will stay with it and you'll stay with us until we're ready to fly.

I am not one of your students at Carver, but I am honored to be one of your chosen "children." That's what you call us, Black and white kids alike, whom you have brought under your wing. Scores of students benefit so much from your guidance as you encourage and support their transitions from high school. You are proving instrumental in changing the lives of many young people. What a tremendous effort. What a tremendous legacy.

Whenever you introduce me to someone, you say, "This white girl doesn't see skin color." The truth is, I do. Let's be honest: don't we all? Just as we take note of other defining characteristics like gender and body type. I believe it's what we do with that information that matters. We are so often wrong when we jump to quick conclusions about others. We are always wrong when we sit in judgment. The difference you see in me is my willingness to cross the lines of race and relationship, to challenge the rules, assumptions and biases.

I used to think that if we all just tried hard enough, wrongs would be set right, peace would prevail and love would overcome. You've helped me understand that my ideologies are absurdly naive but you've taught me to never stop trying to set things right.

Thank you for being my second mother, my North Star.

SEM

Faye L. Williams
Central High School
Class of 1972

Growing up in an all-Black neighborhood, my only encounters with white people were police officers coming through in their old black and white cars, usually to harass us about being off the street by dark, or the couple who bought coupons that we kids clipped from newspapers and magazines. Around four or five on Thursdays they came to a house on the corner of

Ashland and Mosby in the medical district. What that white couple did with those coupons remains a mystery.

April 4, 1968, was a typical day, children roller skating – my favorite pastime – or bike riding, perhaps being chased by a couple of friendly mutts. Grownups were either coming home from work or putting the finishing touches on supper.

We kids were heading home around six that evening when a boy who was known to tell fibs began shouting. He was screaming that the young preacher, in town to help the striking sanitation workers, had been shot. "Boy, you better stop lying!" was our collective cry. I ran the entire block to my house, burst through the door and breathlessly tried to tell my mother this awful news. On the phone with a friend, she said to me, "Girl, don't play with me like that!"

My mother quickly hung up the phone and turned on the news (the same local network that I would later produce for over three decades) to verify what nobody wanted to believe. She collapsed on our front porch and other women left their kitchens to gather in shock and grief. The sound of sirens blared and chaos erupted. When someone set fire to the field next to our house, the fire department arrived, escorted by big National Guard trucks, the soldiers' rifles fixed with bayonets!

This newsreel was playing out in my front yard, insulting the sensibilities of a thirteen-year-old girl. I was just learning about non-violence and now the principled man who championed it was dead from a sniper's bullet. Wait, what?

The next reel of this movie unfolds four months later, when the new school year starts. Carnes Elementary had seen me through eighth grade and I was about to enter Bellevue Junior High. This would be my first interpersonal mingling with white people, and because emotions were still quite raw in the *city, the phases of integration had to be taken in small bits. But there we were, despite not feeling welcomed by many of our white classmates.*

Against all odds, a white girl, Shelley, who sat next to me in homeroom, quickly became a forever friend. Our friendship blossomed as we matriculated into Central High School, surviving the bigotry of folks who opposed crossing racial lines. We endured the typical nuances of teenage life: good grades, pep rallies for games, boys who played those games, break-ups with those boys, etc. In the tenth grade, we and our friends faced suspension when we protested for our right to wear pantsuits to school.

I was proud to be part of "The People Power Project," a panel composed of Black, white, Latino and Jewish students from across the city. Our purpose was to share personal encounters with bigotry and their effects on us. We got positive feedback from local papers and from some of our audiences. For sure, this group helped me navigate the muddy waters of prejudice and racism.

My friendship with Shelley outlasted the hatred that became threats against her and her family. Out of an abundance of caution, we had to stop seeing each other outside of school. When my folks asked me why we didn't see Shelley around anymore, I created excuses, thinking that the truth would keep us apart even after the madness subsided. But it didn't subside. Shelley ended up leaving school after the eleventh grade, before we could create graduation and other teenage-into-young adulthood memories. I am truly sorry for that. But I'm grateful that we seamlessly reconnected years later.

At age seventeen, I registered to vote in Central High School's lobby. This girl who was listed at birth as Colored and known subsequently as Negro, Black, African American and Person of Color, cast her first vote for Presidential candidate, New York Congresswoman Shirley Chisholm in 1972 and, some forty-eight years later, proudly voted for Senator Kamala Harris for the second highest office in the land.

CHAPTER EIGHT

See You in September

Dwain and I survived the traumatic months that framed the second half of our eighth grade school year, but we were both sent packing that summer by parents who now had even greater reason to fear for our safety. Our relationship invited too much scrutiny in a city at a racial crossroads.

Shelley, Laramie summer, 1968

He spent the summer with family in Chicago and I flew to Wyoming. Even though my grandparents in Laramie were aware that I was dating a Black student, the subject was politely but awkwardly avoided during my visit. That is, until one of them, who prided herself on being a devout Christian, could no longer hold back.

"Shelley, you'll go to hell for dating 'Colored' boys."

She echoed the same sentiments when I later married a Jewish man. Racism and self righteousness didn't square at all with my concept of religion; that comment may well have marked the moment when the disconnects between church teachings and flawed human behavior became disappointingly apparent to me. The above exchange pretty well ruined the remainder of my Wyoming summer and I began counting the days until my return flight.

Back in Memphis, I quickly began to understand that Dr. King's murder had ushered in an inevitable surge of radicalism in the Black community. In killing the Black community's preeminent spokesman on April 4, the shooter had succeeded in driving an even deeper wedge between Black and white Americans. Distrust that had historically existed between the two communities now felt like an irreparable breach. Dwain and I didn't stand a chance in this charged environment.

We dated in eighth grade just like any other young people. We were teenagers who fell for each other as only thirteen-year-olds can and for a moment in time we fell hard. It really is as simple as that. Except that he was Black and I was white. We weren't color blind; of course we knew that in our universe no one looked like us. Some of our closest friends doubted our sincerity and our motivations. Would these suspicions and accusations have been raised had race not been a factor? I think not. Granted, most crushes that begin at age thirteen don't enjoy significant longevity. However, from my standpoint, it was the tenor of the place and time and others' perceptions that made our decision messy, complicated and ultimately untenable.

Today, an increasing number of television and magazine advertisements portray interracial couples representing an array of fusion. I understand that such ads spring from a corporate need to enhance the all-important bottom line, but because of my personal history, the images are welcome and important reminders of just how much America has evolved in the past fifty years. And yet, as much as we might wish for an uncomplicated celebration of couples and families of mixed races and ethnicities, it's clear that they continue to face enormous societal challenges and biases.

The Letter

Dear Shelley,

I apologize for not calling you after my return from Chicago. I've gone through a lot of changes since school let out last spring that are difficult to express or explain. Given Dr. King's assassination, I'm in a very different place than I was when we started going out.

I know you missed me this summer as much as I missed you and I had every intention of picking up where we left off in June. I'm not sure it's important to detail all the reasons why, but I feel it would be foolish for us to continue dating, given the climate in Memphis. My decision really has nothing to do with who you are as a person. This is about me and my life going forward. I'm sorry for the hurt this will cause. I hope we can remain friends. I really do wish you all the best.

Dwain

Stand by Me

Dwain,

Your note wasn't a complete surprise, because we haven't spoken since we both got back from our respective "vacations." That doesn't make it any easier to read. I know about the wounds, the pain, and the anger. I get it. Even from my white-girl vantage point,

I'm hurting and angry, too.

In the wake of what we've lived through this past year, I need you more than ever – in my corner, at my back, by my side. At a time when what you need most is to move on. I don't know if you can no longer justify dating a white girl or if you're just not that into me anymore. It doesn't matter.

You and I walked through doors with each other that would probably never have been opened to us had we not dated. There are so many layers to our experiences with each other, our families and friends. I honestly don't know where to go from here. You see, I've crossed over. There is no middle ground for me, no in between. It's either/or, given the predominance of social segregation in Memphis. I've seen and heard and felt too much to pass as just another white girl living in a safe and proscribed world. This is a tremendous time of reckoning for me.

You and I weren't afforded the luxury of a simple teenage crush. Our decision to date each other thrust us unwittingly into an adult realm of complication and concern. We never even had the heady freedom of walking down the street hand in hand or of attending a school dance together. Our affection for one another immediately became a problem, a liability. A personal danger. In a better time and place, who knows? Feels like this is gonna hurt for a long time.

SEM

Dwain J. Kyles
Central High School
Class of 1972

Dwain, Central High Senior, 1972

I turned thirteen years old in August of 1967, just in time for my transition to Bellevue Junior High School. Having spent the previous three years directly across the street at Bruce Elementary, I couldn't wait to do exciting, cool things, including changing classes and playing organized sports.

My family's first years in Memphis posed a significant contrast to the Chicago's Westside neighborhood we'd just left. On our Chicago block at Campbell Park and Oakley Streets, were neighbors who spoke English, Spanish, Italian and Chinese. I played with their children and ate dinner in their homes. When we moved to Memphis, the differences were stark. I saw few white people in our neighborhood, and the ones I did see weren't particularly friendly. Some

Memphis shop windows still posted signs prohibiting entrance or patronizing by "Coloreds." When we attended the "white" movie theater downtown, we had to sit in the balcony. When we learned that Black Memphians could only go to the zoo on Thursdays, my parents decided that, if we couldn't go to the zoo any day of the week, we wouldn't go at all.

The activism of my parents, both of whom grew up in Chicago, framed my budding worldview. The racism and discrimination we experienced in our new hometown must have been even more shocking to them than it was to us, their children. In Memphis, my father was pastor of a small church, recently split from a larger well-established congregation. Our first church "home" was a former funeral parlor at 50 South Parkway West. The tight-knit membership of the Monumental Church became my extended family and the most significant part of my young life. Those members formed a protective cocoon around us, cushioning my siblings and me from the unfamiliar social disparities we often encountered when we left our neighborhood.

I spent first and second grade at Cummings Elementary, within walking distance from our home at the corner of Greenwood and McLemore Streets. The teachers and students all looked like me and shared my social and cultural construct. I had a great time there. At recess and after school, I filled my time with games: dodgeball, baseball, basketball, marbles and spinning tops. When allowed, I enjoyed evening television programs like "Lassie," "Donna Reed," "My Three Sons," and "The Rifleman."

As I was entering second grade, however, my world started to change. My sister, Dwania, was starting first grade as one of the "Memphis 13," a group of students integrating Memphis public elementary schools as part of a local and national effort. I wasn't happy about her going to Bruce Elementary instead of joining me at Cummings. However, focused on my own comfortable second grade experiences, I wasn't very cognizant of the trauma that my younger sister must have felt – so young and vulnerable in a strange place, surrounded by ignorant white adults and silly, mean kids.

When I learned that, as a third grader, I would be joining my sister at Bruce Elementary, I started to pay more attention to Dwania's school experiences and what was happening in our city. What I saw wasn't pretty. Even as young kids, we were aware of the agitation that our parents were feeling; the racist landscape in Memphis was the focal point of the many meetings they attended. However, I don't remember being afraid; I had been around white kids before in Chicago and naively believed that my experience at Bruce Elementary would be similar. I was in for a big surprise.

I soon learned that many white Memphians not only spoke with a funny accent, but that they also seemed to have a problem with kids who looked like me. All too often, I had to defend myself, but thanks to my white third-grade teacher, Mrs. Mary Evans, I was sheltered from much of the drama. She was a joyful, committed and very capable teacher who tolerated no nonsense from any of her students, Black or white.

I quickly formed a close alliance with Kelvin Willis, the other Black kid in my classroom, a friendship that has lasted a lifetime. Thanks to Mrs. Evans' watchful oversight, I also formed lasting relationships with a number of my other classmates – just like old times in Chicago. Tommy Davis, who was white, sometimes invited us to his house for milk and cookies. Other friends included Phillip Lewis, Jewish; Paul Lee, Chinese; Marc Martinez, Hispanic; and two white girls: Cathy Blakeslee and Carol Fancher, who ultimately married Jimmy Fox, one of my best friends at Bellevue Junior High.

Within the protected environment of Mrs. Evans' third grade room, diverse friendships and intellect were allowed to flourish, even in the midst of some of the most racially tumultuous times in American history. In a quiet, understated way, her fearless opposition to the forces of bigotry helped forge a path of peaceful transition. Even though we Black students had to navigate the waters of discrimination, we developed strong relationships with classmates and teachers. Mrs. Evans was raising leaders whose camaraderie set the tone for the student body. We knew that great recommendations from her and other teachers would follow us to Bellevue. By the time we were sixth graders, Bruce Elementary – the school that, for decades, had educated privileged white kids – was a changed institution. Mrs. Evans, who also taught both of my sisters, Dwania and Drusheena, never received enough credit for all she did for our family, but she knew that we loved her.

As I entered Bellevue, I became acutely aware of the differences between my diverse school days and life in my Black neighborhood. I was learning to create and manage something of a dual personality. We Black students were called upon to act as "ambassadors," to help redefine the historic relationships between Memphis' Black and white communities and doing so often compelled us to lead binary lives in order to find acceptance in both environments.

Having lived in a diverse Chicago community, making these adjustments was probably easier for me than for many of my Black friends. Most of them had very little experience with white folks or ethnic diversity. I often found myself trying to help mediate and explain differences between our distinct cultures. That role took on greater significance at Bellevue, when I was elected the first Black student government president in the school's history.

Racist behaviors at school disrupted our otherwise relatively peaceful existence. Inexplicably, the shop teacher at Bellevue had me placed in a remedial classroom, though I knew that I didn't belong there. My parents raised hell with the principal, which set the tone for their dynamics with school officials. Teachers and administrators soon learned that if I saw something, I would say something and, more often than not, my parents would have my back. My tendencies to speak out about discrimination, even if not being visited upon me personally, led to negotiations with the principal about "quiet" resolutions. So began my life of advocacy and a career in law.

While maintaining honor roll grades, singing in the church choir and joining my family in civil rights actions, I also became a starter on Bellevue's football, basketball, baseball and track teams. This was my life, my normal. I loved

Coach Brooks, a dyed-in-the-wool white southerner who taught me to cuss like a sailor. Some of my best times were spent with teammates Jimmy Fox and Jimmy Calandruccio, both white, and Carl Norvell, who is Black. We played every sport together for three years and, whether we were together on the field, on the court or out for pizza, we were brothers, inseparable. We always stuck up for each other when faced with slight or overt episodes of discrimination.

At Bellevue, we met kids who had attended other elementary schools. I'd had my share of "girlfriends" throughout my early years, beginning with Maria, whom I'd walked home from kindergarten in Chicago. In elementary school, I'd had plenty of crushes on girls.

Shelley Moore was different. She wasn't a native Southerner, which meant that she didn't have "that" accent. She was really smart and kind and had a warm smile and bright, lively eyes. Shelley was white. She didn't stand out to me because she was flamboyant or forceful. Though not fearful, she seemed quiet, almost shy. I can't remember when I first noticed her, but I do recall our exchanging corny notes. At age thirteen, we somehow managed to forge the most unlikely relationship from two very different cultural backgrounds. The controversy around our decision to "go steady" may have contributed to her being my first serious girlfriend and the challenges we faced made us even more determined to make our relationship work. So, there we were, dating each other in 1967, in the midst of overarching racial upheaval – at the same time that I was dealing with my own internal conflicts about racial identity and philosophy.

Shelley's father worked in city administration and my father was an active civil rights leader. My family was involved in any number of marches, demonstrations, boycotts and sit-ins. Our parents, who knew of each other, were scared to death as we openly defied cultural mores at such a volatile time. Despite the stakes involved, our parents were very understanding. We were intelligent young people but we couldn't be swayed by the rational fears voiced by our families and friends.

Not only did my best Black male friends ask me if I was crazy, but Black girls expressed their displeasure and concern for my safety. For the first time, I was forced to challenge my own commitment to the civil rights movement, my own identity and my life purpose. Was I "selling out," as some in my social circle suggested? Was I undermining my own reputation as a spokesperson for Black students who had been the driving force in my election as student council president? Was I insulting my own sisters and other Black girls by making such a choice? Pretty weighty stuff for a thirteen-year-old, but, even then, I took these issues very seriously.

On April 4, 1968, everything changed when Dr. Martin Luther King, Jr. was murdered in downtown Memphis. Prior to his assassination, I had struggled with whether I believed that, in the quest for freedom, the methods of Malcolm X or Stokely Carmichael might be better than the peaceful resistance promoted by Dr. King.

While at baseball practice on the afternoon of April 4, I knew something was terribly wrong when I was told to leave the field and get dressed. A church member would soon be arriving to pick me up. Air raid horns were blaring and the sound of sirens filled the air. Dr. King and others were expected for dinner at our home that night, but I didn't immediately make the connection between the chaos and our evening plans. By the time I got home, everything became clear. Church members who had spent the day setting up the dining room and cooking the feast were now huddled in our home, crying and whispering.

My mother broke the news to me. She explained that my father had been near Dr. King on the motel balcony when he was shot. Without cell phones, we were in the dark, consumed by uncertainty and anxiety, not even certain that the attack was over. My siblings and I had never seen adults so deeply affected. We were scared, my own fear amplified by fury. How could this happen? How could this man of peace be shot down like a dog?!

I have not been the same since that day. I knew that I had to become an activist, to choose sides. I didn't make any pronouncements; I simply decided to change my outlook on how I would live my life, though it didn't happen overnight. In protest, I resigned my position as student council president because the school administration refused to deal with issues important to Bellevue's Black students. I was still playing sports and remained close to my white teammates, but I constantly thought about extricating myself from relationships that seemed to contradict my new path. I had to learn how to navigate "their" world while helping liberate my people. I couldn't allow myself to be too close to white people. They were not to be trusted. Period. My relationship with Shelley, which had become harder and harder for me to reconcile, began to deteriorate. At age fourteen, I couldn't accurately explain why I pulled away, so I made excuses and allowed the space between us to grow. The truth is, I never stopped caring about her. I simply couldn't reconcile the dichotomy. Thankfully, our renewed deep and abiding affection for each other remains strong to this day.

At Central High School, my activism ramped up. We Black students protested the administration's seemingly endless onslaught of biased decisions and actions: the bigotry of teachers, the absence of a curriculum that spoke to our heritage and the paucity of Black teachers and administrators. Our protests led to a formal student walkout that attracted the news media as we marched to the Board of Education. I reluctantly quit playing sports because of the racist tendencies of Central's coaches and players – Coach Cate in particular. As a consequence of dropping ROTC, my buddy, Don Jones, and I were not issued diplomas or allowed to walk with our graduating class. I spent most of my time during and after school with my closest friends, Kelvin, Don and Theron "Popsy" Northcross. We did everything together.

Though we lost Popsy a few years ago, the rest of us remain close today, staying in touch and supporting each others' lives and dreams. As I continue on this journey, I reflect upon my experiences and the people who have patiently helped me navigate these difficult waters, back to a person who is not disillusioned, able to trust and believe that we really are all in this together. I have been blessed with the most supportive relationships and have been fortunate that my friends and family have accepted me as I am, despite my mistakes. For this, I am truly grateful.

CHAPTER NINE

Just My Imagination

Central High School, Memphis

And then came the tenth grade. Established in 1909 as Memphis' flagship high school, Central was known as " The High School." Located just two blocks north of Bellevue Junior High, it remains another revered Memphis institution.

I was happy to leave behind what felt like the confines of junior high school, to finally be free of Bellevue's archaic rules. At the very least, boys and girls shared Central's entrances, stairways and lunchroom seating. However, I felt somewhat uneasy about entering a new school as a freshman, once again following Lissa, who was entering eleventh grade, and Bob, now a senior. I had the changing of classes down and figured I could probably keep up academically, but I had other concerns that fall of 1969. Not only did my siblings precede me but now my reputation and predilections would also be a factor with teachers, administrators and fellow students. It would be difficult for anyone to overlook the fact that my circle of friends was Black, including my boyfriend, Carl.

I foolishly thought that a larger and slightly older student body might offer a kinder and gentler response to those of us who dared do things differently, to those of us who could not, would not, among other things, pledge our allegiance to the echoes of Jim Crow, Dixieland and the Confederacy. I hoped that somewhere in that crowded field I would find a more diverse group of kindred spirits, kids who not only tolerated but actually embraced the notion of interracial friendship and dating.

My fantasies were put in check as I sat in Mrs. Matthews' homeroom on the first day of tenth grade. I listened in disbelief as she proudly shared details of her summer spent with the John Birch Society, a right-wing organization vehemently opposed to any aspect of the civil rights movement, especially social integration. All I could think was, "here we go again." My teacher's unvarnished and clearly unrepentant remarks supported the fact that we were still mired in the past – a past defined by and insistent upon disenfranchising and demeaning people of color and others who didn't fit within history's narrow parameters of white and right. This is the woman in whose classroom I was destined to begin each day of that school year. I'd changed schools when I advanced to Central, but not much had actually shifted socially or politically.

Spring snow, Central High School, 1971

Kim Story
Central High School
Class of 1970

I must preface my reminiscences with a couple of caveats. First, during the period I'm talking about, 1965-1970, I was a poster boy for self-absorption. Even knowing that this doesn't make me unique, it colors all my thoughts and impressions of this time. I was also oblivious to a lot of what was going on in the country. That improved when I moved into high school, as I began to notice things that didn't affect only me. Much of what I know about the history of those times, I have learned since.

I was born in 1952 and grew up in a lower middle-class neighborhood. What we called North Memphis is now known as Smoky City. The neighborhood was full of the type of post-war, small red brick duplexes we lived in from 1952 to 1970. I attended the neighborhood school, Guthrie Elementary, which spanned first through eighth grade. I don't have specific memories of my socialization, especially in terms of race. To give my parents the benefit of the doubt, I think theirs was a fairly subtle, though no less insidious form of prejudice, probably due to the fact that they dealt with African Americans every day in their professional lives. My description of that brand of racism is this: There are two kinds of people. People and Black people. However, my peers' approach ranged from that sort of racism to virulent, N-word hatred. I absorbed it and found myself closer to the latter.

What saved me is the fact that, as a ninth grader in 1966, I changed schools and environments when my parents pulled strings to enroll me in Snowden Junior High. Humes Junior High would have been populated with my elementary school crowd. My new school was located in a different neighborhood and its students fed into Central High. Suddenly, I found myself in a whole new world with students who represented higher societal and, more importantly, educational status. The difference between my years at Guthrie and my experiences at Snowden and Central were, to say the least, eye-opening.

Long story shorter, I remember the day my world, in terms of racism, turned upside down. I made a remark to my best friend that I'm too embarrassed to quote even more than fifty years later. He simultaneously shamed and schooled me. The lesson was powerful and effective. I didn't instantly become Mother Teresa, but a light came on, one just bright enough to show me the path I should follow. That light grew brighter and brighter and by the time integration became a reality, I believe I was ready for it. I probably still saw individuals as Black people, but I know I saw them as people. Thanks to what I had learned and continued to learn, I was able to accept Black students as part of my community. As belonging. As friends.

Every Breath You Take

The Ku Klux Klan and the White Citizens Council shared a singular precept. Although they had no use for Jews, Catholics, Hispanics or Asians, they focused a perverse and absolute hatred on the Black community and white people who befriended or worked with that community. Their history of predatory and egregious behavior was defined by a wide swath of terror, particularly across the American South.

In the 1950s and 1960s, Black and white activists registered voters, occupied buses as Freedom Riders, marched and boycotted together. Some further risked their lives by socializing with, dating or marrying one another. They were among those who were victims of vicious attacks carried out by the Klan and the Council. All too often though, the acts of violence were perpetrated against those whose only crime, tragically, was being Black in the wrong place at the wrong time.

The White Citizens Council was established in 1954 in Mississippi, its membership made up of white-collar businessmen, the "suits." Their ranks included those who worked in banking, insurance, law and medicine. Although its members didn't wear hoods and robes, the Council, often acting as cover for the Klan, was closely tied to that more overtly nefarious group. The Council was purportedly less violent than the Klan, but history has proven that to be factually untrue. Both organizations were unequivocally opposed to desegregation under any circumstance, be it in education, accommodations, or, most significantly, in personal relationships.

Established in 1985, The Council of Conservative Citizens (CCC), is the successor of the White Citizens Council. Through them, the reign of terror continues to this day. Their worst nightmare remains procreative relationships between whites and Blacks, certain to dilute and eventually render impotent and powerless the white race. White supremacy has always been the calling card of such coalitions.

A Whiter Shade Of Pale

Bill,

You know my face and my name, but you don't know me. You only know that you don't like me because of the people I hang out with. I know your face and your name, too, and I actually know some dirty little details about you. I hear you boast about your "connections." Who exactly are you connected to? The Klan? The Council? Who is your daddy, Bill? Who's your grandpa, uncle, cousin? Are you all connected?

Yesterday, I had the displeasure of passing you and a group of visitors on a staircase. Why you've been chosen to represent the school as tour guide is beyond me. When I walked by, you practically spit out your words:

"This is Shelley, our resident n****r lover."

Congratulations! You got everyone's attention. Do you really have nothing better to do than harass and threaten me? Your bravado makes you little more than an insidious bedbug that leaves behind the itch and scarring of its sinister infestation.

I'm connected, too, Bill. To the difference between right and wrong, good and evil. You are neither right nor good.

SEM

Who the hell was this guy Bill and why was he tagging me? Even if I could have connected the dots, what could I have done about it? Who would have taken my accusations seriously? In those days, blatant harassment in school, especially race-based harassment, wasn't considered a punishable offense. In fact, teachers and administrators usually turned a blind eye to such behavior. Acting the bully wasn't a new phenomenon, but "bullying" had not yet surfaced as the popular term for particularly offensive and potentially dangerous behavior. Today, we recognize how harmful such affronts can prove, especially in the lives of young people.

The brave letter I penned to Bill didn't accurately represent my true feelings. Those were really unsettling times for me as a freshman in high school. I fully understood that many if not most white folks in my greater orbit didn't condone my choice of friends or who to date. Even though I was acutely aware of the fact that Black students were far more accustomed than I to ridicule, name calling and worse on a regular basis, that understanding, that perspective did little to quell my personal anxiety.

I had no idea how much worse things could get.

House of the Rising Sun

Our second floor black rotary phone rested in a nook, just across the hall from the bedroom I shared with Lissa. On any given weekday in our house on Vance, the Moore family was barely stirring at 6:30 a.m. The phone call at that hour signaled an emergency. As the sun rose that morning, darkness descended on our home.

I answered that call, and was addressed by an unfamiliar voice:

"Is this Shelley?"

"Yes it is."

"Let me talk to your mother."

With more than a little trepidation, I called my mom to the phone. My mind raced as I slipped back under the covers, certain that I had committed some terrible offense at school. The man knew my name. But why the early phone call? Listening from my room, I could tell that Sonya sounded increasingly agitated.

As usual, the five of us gathered a short time later for a breakfast that would normally have consisted of cereal or bacon and eggs or pancakes. I don't recall. I do know that no food reached my mouth that morning. It was obvious that something was terribly wrong and that, somehow, the turmoil involved me. My parents proceeded to give us an account of the horrifying phone call, which on the caller's end went like this:

"Mrs. Moore, this is the White Citizens Council. I just bought a shotgun. I will use it to blow your daughter's head off unless she stops dating 'n*****s.' I'm watching her."

The details of his call were mind boggling and chilling to say the least. Blow my head off because I dated Black students? How could a grown man target a teenager with such an ominous threat? Unimaginable. This had to be a dream, a terrifying nightmare that was happening to someone else. A piece of fiction to read or watch on a screen.

"I'm never going to school again."

"You absolutely will be going to school. For the foreseeable future, one of us will drive the three of you to and from school. Walking on either side of you, Bob and Lissa will effectively serve as bodyguards as you enter and exit the school building."

This exchange didn't sit well with the three of us kids. I questioned how my siblings' presence would impede my being shot or prevent one of them from being injured or killed as an unintended target. Lissa was particularly reluctant and displeased with her sudden and involuntary involvement in my mess. Bob knew that, as my big brother, he was expected to assume a protective role. Regardless of our opinion about this scenario, we all did what we were told. As the days dragged on, my imagination calcified into sheer terror.

Except for attending school, I was put into virtual seclusion, which, for a socially active teenager, might as well have been a sentence to solitary confinement. My parents laid down the law: I was not to be seen outside of school with any of my friends and I was not to discuss the phone call with anyone. So, I placed friendships and dating on hold without notice or much explanation. A lot of tears were shed those nights when my head finally hit the pillow.

Following up on the threat, my dad met first with Central's principal who did absolutely nothing in response. He also met with the Police Commissioner who promised an increased squad patrol in our neighborhood. Police cars began cruising our street, their unusual presence bringing an odd mixture of anxiety and a sense of relief. As a family, we took it in, hunkered down and hoped for the best, which in hindsight seems a bit nuts.

I don't know how anyone could have tracked the caller or effectively protected me from his threat but I might have felt a little better if the authorities had at least taken the situation seriously and tried to intervene. On the other hand, considering the authorities at the time, maybe not. I was absolutely sure that a sharpshooter – righteous, armed and loaded – was stationed on a building rooftop waiting for the opportunity to kill me.

I'd endured years of both callous and quiet disapproval, but nothing had prepared me for this degree of personal danger, the sense of having a target on my back, the horror of being stalked. Was this man a lone wolf or did he really represent the White Citizens Council? Were there students at Central who were complicit in this threat?

When the alarm clock rang on school mornings, I just wanted to pull the covers over my head, hoping that one day I would wake up to realize this was all a bad dream. School days evaporated in a haze of dread and paranoia. I was a mess.

In the Still of the Night

Night Rider,

You know very well that the dark of night wraps me in a shroud of fear these days. Why did you choose a visitation just when it would hurt the most, when the fine lines between dreams and reality blur? Because of the coward who threatened my life, sleep doesn't come easily, and when it does, it's fitful and shallow. I only feel safe because my sister is in the next bed, my parents and brother across the hall.

That sense of comfort and protection abandoned me when you appeared last night. I don't understand how you got into our house and up the stairs without being heard, but you clearly startled my sister when she yelled out to a figure standing in our bedroom doorway. "Who are you? What are you doing here? What do you want?"

Lying with my back to the door, I was frozen in place, holding my breath, imagining that a gun was aimed straight at me. Was a man standing by my bed? Was I about to die? Papers rustled on the table between our beds. And then, utter silence. I'm not sure which was louder: the stillness in the room or the deafening roar between my ears. I didn't move for hours. When the sun came up, I finally found the courage to turn over in bed. I couldn't begin to imagine what the day might bring.

Lissa had no idea what I was talking about when I recounted the night's events. Nothing. She suggested that I'd had a nightmare. Actually, you used her to channel your menacing threat. No figment of my imagination, I heard the terror in her voice and I'll never forget her words. I now have to carry the load of that singular experience in a shared room. Well done.

SEM

Of course, no one, with or without a weapon, stood in our bedroom door that night. Had an intruder been able to gain access to our secure house, had he actually made it as far as our room and had he aimed a gun at me from a few feet away, this book would not have been written. He surely would have accomplished his mission. I, and perhaps others in my family, would have died that night. The timing and trauma of my sister's nightmare was not only extraordinary, but was also the last thing my psyche and heart needed at that moment. I had to continually convince myself that I wasn't losing my mind.

You Gotta Move

In the spring of 1970, my parents decided to leave our home of eight years and move our family into a sixth-floor apartment on Central Avenue. In the wake of Dr. King's assassination, the threat on my life and considering Jerry's position with the city, they felt that our family was too vulnerable, too visible and too accessible in a stand-alone house. With the move came an unpublished phone number and address, granting us at least the illusion of increased safety and security. All of us had grown weary of being on high alert and under police protection. Bob would soon be off to college, giving my folks even more reason to downsize. Even though I had mixed emotions about leaving our home, I soon grew to love the more cosmopolitan dwelling – especially because it came with a community swimming pool. No small detail considering the heat of Memphis summers.

Out of an abundance of caution, my parents continued to strictly monitor and restrict my social life. But, they knew it wasn't feasible to indefinitely keep me under lock and key. I was restless and ready to have my life back. My confinement was eventually eased and then lifted, though with strict rules and curfews in place.

CHAPTER TEN

Saturday in the Park

Overton Park is nothing less than a Midtown Memphis treasure, our "Central Park." In the late 1800s and early 1900s, Memphis claimed the title of Hardwood Capital of the World with thirty-two operational lumber mills. Careless management ultimately wiped out many of Memphis' largest stands of deciduous trees. Overton Park's 342 acres include one of the few remaining old growth forests in Tennessee. In 1936, as part of the Works Progress Administration, a performance venue was constructed in Overton Park.

In the early 1970s, engineers submitted a design for the Memphis portion of Interstate 40, a major artery spanning the continent from California to North Carolina. Overton Park was in the crosshairs of urban renewal, as the new highway was designed to bisect its acreage. A group of civic-minded Midtowners launched an heroic and ultimately victorious legal effort to contest that plan. Their proposal saved the precious resource by rerouting the throughway to skirt the park's perimeter. The group's lawsuits, initially given little chance of success, were ultimately heard by the Supreme Court. With its decision, the future of the park was secure.

Overton Park Shell

The Shell was also saved by the bell with the final design of the interstate. Symphony orchestras, opera and ballet companies have performed on its open-air stage. Elvis, Aaron Neville, Roseanne Cash, Booker T. and the MGs, Emmy Lou Harris, Mavis Staples and countless others have entertained crowds from its platform. Today, the Shell offers fifty free shows each year between June and October. The setting is spectacular and scheduled events find hundreds of Memphians enjoying an evening under the stars.

The apartment on Central is where I spent my junior year. I slowly reclaimed my freedom, enjoying an expanded social life that, for the first time in years, included a couple of white friends. Ours was a diverse circle of fun-loving and stubbornly principled young people. In an era rife with political and social action, we regularly participated in school protests and city-wide demonstrations.

Weekend nights often found us seated on the concrete bleachers at the Shell enjoying live music; free days, we engaged in fierce and hilarious tennis competitions or listened to the newest cool album in someone's living room. On particularly adventurous evenings, we sat on downtown bluffs watching burdened, illuminated river barges slowly make their way north to the source of the Mississippi or south to "Nawlins."

Following Dr. King's assassination, retail and commercial districts were abandoned and shuttered, as palpable fear and anxiety continued to haunt the city. Downtown Memphis became a literal ghost town as large department stores that had long defined Main Street either went out of business or moved their brick and mortar operations to East Memphis. Overton Square, a hip Midtown dining and shopping district, was similarly deserted. The tinges of social integration that had begun appearing publicly were once again moved indoors for private gatherings or abandoned altogether.

Don Jones
Central High School
Class of 1972

Don, 1970

My parents, my brother and I were native Chicagoans. During my childhood, it never occurred to me that we would move to the South. Why would we? As a boy, my impression of the South was that of a place of racism, oppression and intolerance.

So, you can imagine that it scared the hell out of me when I found out we were moving to Memphis...and only ninety days after the death of Dr. King.

Our family had lived for the previous five years in an interracial enclave in a Chicago suburb that can only be described as unique. At its founding just after World War II, the York Center Community Cooperative, known as the Co-op, was a multicultural experiment in cooperative living. Indeed, in the fifties and sixties, most would consider this amalgamation of races and religions somewhat radical. For kids growing up in our one-hundred-acre community with its one-acre lots, wide-open spaces and left-leaning values, it was fantastic.

The Co-op provided a nurturing haven. We ran and played from one home to the next, secure in the feeling of complete safety. From the third grade through junior high school, I enjoyed the peace and harmony of a place that lived the values to which many Americans of the 1960s aspired. My buddies were Black, white, Asian and Jewish and, in the main, we were largely oblivious to the often-violent societal changes going on in the world around us. By the time I was thirteen and had moved through Cub Scouts and Little League, snowball fights and treehouses to the brink of teenage years, my life in the cocoon of the Co-op with its mix of races and religions was a known quantity to me and, by and large, quite comfortable. As a thirteen-year-old in 1968, I felt uneasy about the reality of moving to Memphis and what lay ahead.

Nothing in my experience prepared me for the spring of 1968, when, after the school year was over, we moved to Memphis, Tennessee. The farthest south I had ever been was down-state, to Springfield, and certainly not below the Mason-Dixon Line. At the time, I didn't really hear the word Memphis. My adolescent's mind's eye keyed on the word, Tennessee. I envisioned a strange place with dirt roads, women in bare feet and children in straw hats. Little did I know that I would come to love Memphis and make lifelong friendships there. In fact, in many ways, I would come to think of Memphis as home.

After a miserable ninth-grade year at Christian Brothers High School, I settled into Central High with a close group of friends. In fact, they were friends who would become like brothers, and we have remained so all of our lives. After school, we played ball and on Friday and Saturday nights, we looked forward to house parties.

Some tentative friendships, which rarely extended outside of school, formed with white kids. Then there was Shelley. The best way I can describe Shelley is to say that, even as a teen, she possessed maturity and self-assurance uncommon at any age. It allowed her to be comfortable enough in her own skin to cultivate real relationships with Black kids. Sometimes it seemed she was fighting the demons of conventional behavior and protocol all by herself. I admired her for that. In hindsight, it was a tribute to her parents. Her family would've loved the Co-op.

One Friday night, the party was at Shelley's house with a mix of Black and white students in attendance. There was music, dancing and food and there was also a lot of fellowship and good feelings among all present. The evening had begun to wind down and the room was dark. It must have been about eleven o'clock, and midnight curfews were looming for most of us. As we sat in a circle on the living room floor, "Bridge Over Troubled Water" by Simon and Garfunkel was playing on the record player, and kids were just talking, very openly and honestly about whatever came to mind. The scene reminded me so much of the Co-op. Kids just talking and getting to know one another as humans. Not Black ones or white ones, just humans, sharing a space and a moment. When the lights came back on and people began to leave, I looked at Shelley and I smiled. I don't think she understood what I was smiling about, but then again, perhaps she did.

Angry Young Man

The year was 1969. We teenagers watched and listened as stories of unrest on campuses across the country found their way into the local news. The issues of the day rang especially true with some of us at Central, inspiring an uptick of relatively mild rebelliousness. We protested school rules and traditions that felt woefully dated, irrelevant and unnecessarily rigid. Of course, we thought our impatience and anger was productive and righteous. Feeling boxed in and needlessly restricted, we simply wanted the reins loosened a bit so that we could more freely express our individualism. We insisted that the stylistic and cultural freedoms we sought wouldn't diminish our commitment to academics.

A small group of white boys, my brother included, faced suspension when their hair touched shirt collars. Black boys and girls began to sport impressive Afros. ROTC instructors were particularly displeased with the look of military hats perched on the lofty do's. After having been on the receiving end of far too many lectures from teachers and administrators about personal style choices, my long, untamed hair was thankfully off limits. For this girl, plastic curlers were a thing of the past.

After several of us were sent home for intentionally violating the dress code, Central's administration finally relented. Boys were allowed to wear blue jeans and slacks were green-lighted for girls. The following year girls were also allowed to wear jeans. I loved finally being able to go to school in my denim bell bottoms and leather sandals, an updated look that was a far cry from the pleated skirts, matching sweaters, knee socks and loafers that had dominated my Bellevue wardrobe.

Denim jackets also became commonplace, sporting buttons that voiced popular sentiments:

"War is not Healthy for Children and other Living Things..."

"Free Angela..."

"Black is Beautiful..."

"Give Peace a Chance..."

"Respect Yourself..."

Liberal white kids and activist Black kids were a thorn in the side of white jocks and the white fraternity and sorority cultures that had long held court over Central's student body. Interactions between differing factions were generally tempered but an undercurrent of smoldering tension lingered, with occasional clashes on the school grounds.

In recent years, a number of my former white classmates have remarked that they were oblivious to any degree of conflict or even any simmering unrest between Black and white students at Bellevue and Central. Having spent the same years in those institutions, it's inconceivable to me that my white counterparts were largely unmindful of the ways that Black students struggled to be fully recognized and heard. That disparity in our collective memory illustrates the compartmentalization of our lives and our school experiences. Clearly, we were all products of the prevailing winds of home and community.

In our day, junior high incorporated grades seven through nine; high school, grades ten through twelve. Unlike my years at Bellevue, I was no honor student at Central. Though I managed to keep my head above the academic waters, I was admittedly more distracted and less focused on my education. Two classroom moments in particular stand out for me when I reflect on those years.

As a freshman at Central, I wrote a paper in English class based on Neil Young's *After the Goldrush*. Other than the fact that I liked the song, I can't recall the nature of the assignment, why I chose those lyrics to expound upon or what message I hoped to convey. I figured I'd ruffle a feather or two and roll the dice. Well, you could have knocked me over with one of those feathers when Miss Middleton gave my paper an A+!

My other distinct classroom memory isn't quite as pleasant. At a time when America was embroiled in an extremely controversial war, my American History teacher was an army veteran. Many Americans were of the opinion that the engagement in Vietnam was a cruel and unnecessary war. Adults opposed to the war undoubtedly had far more developed convictions than we students, but the lives of teenagers were on the line, and the impending draft presented a nagging and terrifying prospect to many of our family members and friends.

My classmate Marva and I spent hours arguing with our teacher about the morality of the conflict and the horrors that were being inflicted upon not only troops but also innocent victims caught in the crossfire. The "D" I received in that class, my first and last such grade, was hard earned.

Barbara Birge
Central High School
Class of 1972

I've never had a good memory, and my recollections of Central float unfocused like a disjointed dream. Events largely escape me, but certain faces and facts persist.

There's the fact, for instance, that a considerable portion of eleventh-grade English class was spent on the study of two plays by an obscure English playwright, John Drinkwater. They were titled "Abraham Lincoln" and "Robert E. Lee."

Who can wonder that I arrived at college with an embarrassing gap in my knowledge of literature. No Twain, no Hemingway, no Fitzgerald – the list went on. Only in recent years did I realize what surely lay behind this odd curriculum. I have no doubt that our teacher, Evelyn Meeks, wanted to indoctrinate us with her lost-cause perspective on the Civil War. God help us. As Paul Simon sang, "When I think back on all the crap I learned in high school, it's a wonder I can think at all."

Then, there's the fact that when I became editor of our school newspaper, The Warrior, the yearly coveted trip to a journalism conference in New York City was strangely no longer to be. I'll never know for sure, but I strongly suspect our class' racial integration put the kibosh on that long-standing tradition. Our newspaper staff was being integrated, and I'd lay money that no faculty advisor was going to risk accompanying an African American student out of town. As a white woman, I only came to this insight in recent years, largely through conversations with former classmates. I heard heartbreaking accounts of how my African American classmates were refused tutoring by teachers, discriminated against by coaches and ROTC instructors, and denied positions such as editor of The Warrior – yes, the position I was awarded. In 2005, some of us created and gave to Central a homemade documentary about our high school experiences. It is well worth watching. The new perspective I gained through that exercise has caused me to wonder how naive I may still be about our experiences.

Black Monday walkouts were organized by the NAACP to protest the lack of Black representation on the school board, at a time when half of Memphis' public students were Black. At Central, the walkouts were led by Dwain Kyles and other classmates who, on successive Mondays, left school and made their way to the Board of Education building. I distinctly remember Mrs. Meeks locking our classroom door to protect us from those renegade students in the halls.

On the eve of his retirement, principal Robert King charged student leaders with finding a way to make our interracial experience work. As editor of the paper, I was included in that group. As a result of Mr. King's wisdom, we gathered over the summer before our senior year. We entered our senior year with cohesion and a commitment to fairness and, in fact, made it work. That experience was the most important education I could ever have received from Central and for that, I remain deeply grateful.

Brick By Brick

In 1927, an enormous classic art-deco building was constructed on North Cleveland Street in the Crosstown area of Midtown Memphis. Boasting over a million square feet, it housed a Sears catalog, retail and distribution center. Only a couple of miles east of downtown, the Sears building was considered fairly suburban at the time it was built. It now anchors the greater Midtown area, residential and commercial development having pushed the city limits much farther east. Recently, the iconic structure was brilliantly transformed into a mixed-use, live/work community by a group of visionary developers and investors.

Crosstown Concourse, Memphis

Originally destined for demolition after sitting abandoned for some twenty years, an ambitious and audacious dream was spun, financed, undertaken and finally completed in 2017. During the restoration process, I watched for months as skilled workers painstakingly repointed the brickwork mortar on that magnificent building. The building is now known as Crosstown Concourse.

When I was young, the arrival of a Sears catalog brought the promise of birthday or Christmas presents and new school clothes. We kids fought over the tome, turning down its page corners to mark our favorite toys or outfits. Sometimes we were lucky enough to receive items from our wish list. That building holds wonderful memories for scores of Memphians, but it might prove to hold even more promise for the city's future.

One can live, work, dine, exercise and bank within the edifice of the Crosstown Concourse. Clinics provide medical and dental care to the underserved. State of the art kitchen laboratories teach nutrition and cooking skills. Studios and exhibition galleries showcase the work of local artisans. The compositions of live jazz ensembles can often be heard throughout its corridors.

The building is now also home to Crosstown High, a public charter school that enrolls some three hundred students. When classes let out at the end of the school day, students of every conceivable description flow into the public spaces of the building. They are an energetic group of Black, white, Asian, Latino and multiracial kids whose wardrobe choices display a veritable red carpet of eclectic fashion statements. Hairstyles run the gamut of popular trends, from waist-length extensions and elegant braids to butch cuts.

On any given afternoon, I'm only witnessing a quick sampling and cross segment of the school's population, but this much is clear: Crosstown High represents a fully integrated student body, not merely a desegregated institution. There is little doubt that my friends and I would have loved to attend such a school. Watching this wave of synchronistic energy gives me hope. Having endured the tight lines that were strictly maintained in our schools, I'm thrilled that some in this generation have the opportunity to learn in such a dynamic and fluid environment. Our future literally rests on their shoulders.

Carl Norvell

Central High School
Class of 1972

Author's Note:

The following narrative is based solely on an in-person interview I recently conducted with Carl, my dear friend and former classmate. This is his story, raw and unfiltered, which he has asked me to compose on his behalf. I have not embellished or exaggerated his memories. It is remarkable to me that, to this day, Carl does not know self pity or complaint. As close as he and I were as teenagers, I did not know most of the details of his life.

The year was 1960. Tickets in hand, two scared little boys had to be helped up into the passenger car. I was eight, my brother, Daryl, four. When our mom, Arvinzina, finally had enough of married life with our dad, Bill, she headed for California with our eight siblings, leaving Daryl and me in Chicago with Bill. Having neither the desire nor the wherewithal to care for us, Bill bought two train tickets, placed us in our seats and paid a porter to watch over us as we journeyed alone to Memphis. I was going home, having been born at Memphis' John Gaston Hospital in 1952 before moving to Chicago with my folks. Now, I was headed to an unfamiliar house filled with people I didn't know, into a circumstance I could never have imagined.

My kin sometimes took on last names, seemingly at will, usually having to do with a falling out of some nature. When all was said and done, there were too many surnames to keep straight: Norvell, Smith, Johnson, Moore, to name a few. My last name came from my mom's side. To add another element of confusion in our family, we kids looked like we came from different daddies, some of us arriving chocolate-colored, others light-skinned.

When we reached Memphis, Corine Moore took us into her small shotgun house, already burdened with several generations of family. Her boy, Bill, our dad, was quite light, as was my brother, Daryl. To her way of thinking, the lighter the better. Her son could do no wrong, despite the fact that he could hardly be deemed a good husband or dad and despite the fact that he apparently fathered dark children as well as his mother's preferred flavor. Corine favored Daryl and treated me as if I weren't her blood. Almost as if I didn't exist. Certainly as if I didn't matter. I spent the next ten years listening to my grandma tell me that I "was never gonna amount to nuthin."

Corine lived in The Bottom. Washington Bottom, smack in the middle of Midtown Memphis, practically in the shadow of the Sears building and a stone's throw from the Curb Market. The city knew the lane as Washington Avenue, but its residents knew better. It was little more than an alley lined with humble houses on one side and lush overgrowth on the other. I came up in Corine's house, sharing an unlit bedroom with Daryl, which made doing my school work at home impossible. I alone wasn't allowed in the living room, not to do my homework or to join others in front of the television.

My grandma was downright cruel to me. Certain that I was headed for a life of trouble and misfortune, she imposed harsh rules and limits on my daily life. If I got home after her curfew of dusk, I would find the front door locked. No one inside was allowed to let me in, which meant I spent far too many nights sleeping hungry on the front porch or hoping a neighbor would take me in and feed me. I never received a penny from Corine for lunch money or anything else and was lucky to get a serving of oatmeal before heading to school. It didn't take me long to figure out that my chocolate skin was the reason she treated me so bad.

There was never a vehicle associated with Corine's household. We all walked everywhere. Even in the worst weather Memphis could dish out, I walked to and from school with my best friends from The Bottom. To this day, we have annual Washington Bottom reunions, bringing together those of us still living and remembering friends who have passed on. I was enrolled in Maury Elementary, just behind Tech High School on Poplar, a short walk from my new home. It didn't bother me that most of the kids at Maury were white, but I did mind having to repeat third grade, which I'd already completed in Chicago!

I entered seventh grade at Bellevue Junior High and loved the bigger school. Even though I was painfully shy and skinny, Bellevue coaches took note of me and I was soon on the roster for all sports: track, baseball, basketball and football. For three years, I was a starter on every team. Coach Brooks, the football coach, became an important mentor to me right away. He saw my drive and determination, my hunger for competition and the chance to prove myself. Coach developed a training regimen for me and held me to the highest standard as a key player. He also did his best to bulk me up, but the truth was, there just wasn't a reliable enough food source to properly fuel my body and grow it sufficiently. Nobody knew what my home life was like except my buddies from the 'hood and they only knew because I showed up so often at their front doors in search of a meal and a bed.

I became friends, close friends, with my teammates. We had each others' backs, on and off the fields and courts. Sometimes we'd head to a local pizza place after practice; they always covered me when I didn't have money, which was most of the time. No questions asked, no explanation needed. Black and white kids eating together in a restaurant was hardly a common sight in the late 1960s. I only remember being in one actual fight at Bellevue when twin brothers tried to take my lunch money one too many times. Little did they know, I usually didn't have much or any lunch money in my pockets!

The last time they approached me in the hallway, I dared them to meet me in the boy's room. When they showed up, two against one, I hit them upside the head with one of my platform shoes, not hard enough to really inflict harm, but enough to put the fear of God in them. Those shoes were not only stylin', but they also came in pretty handy for self defense. The brothers never tried to rob me again, and in fact, we became friends after that. I did pretty well in my classes and I loved playing sports, especially football. I'd begun to notice girls but schoolwork and athletics always came first. Even at that young age, I knew my future depended on succeeding at both.

In the last half of our ninth-grade year, I asked Shelley out and we started dating. I'd limp to her house from Crump Stadium, my legs cramped up after grueling practices that usually included running the bleachers. Shelley caught my attention with her kindness and her friendliness. The fact that interracial dating was still rare in Memphis didn't stop us; we simply enjoyed the pleasure of each other's company. Unfortunately, when her life was threatened in tenth grade, we had to stop seeing each other and ended up going our separate ways. It's wonderful to be in each others' lives again after all we went through as teenagers.

In my senior year at Bellevue, Central High School coaches began scouting us and encouraging some of us to consider Central over rival Black high schools. Most of us chose Central. I started out playing basketball and football, but I couldn't compete with the taller players on the court. After my successes at Bellevue, I wasn't used to sitting on the bench. Coach Kilpatrick wasn't at all disappointed when I decided to focus solely on football. I wasn't a big guy, but I was powerful and aggressive and I liked to win. Larger opponents often ended up on the ground in a match-up with me. There was noticeable racism in Central sports, some coming from other coaches, some from my teammates. The players soon learned that Coach K wouldn't tolerate racist comments and behaviors. I earned a leadership position on the team, serving as co-captain my junior and senior years and I began to think seriously about my future. All I could figure was that decent grades and football would be my ticket to a better life.

I desperately wanted a way out of The Bottom, away from my grandma. There was no one else to take me in as a minor, so I knew it was on me to figure out a way to make it happen. Coach encouraged me to apply for football scholarships. My dream was to play for Notre Dame, USC or Alabama, but those schools were pure fantasy. I did receive offers from small Black colleges, the University of South Alabama and the U.S. Naval Academy. In fact, the Academy offered me a full four-year scholarship. I'll never understand why Coach moved away from me when I needed him most. I didn't know the first thing about the college system and suddenly I didn't have an advocate. I didn't know where to turn. My dream and I both fell through the cracks. I now know that this happens all the time to qualified kids who lack guidance and sponsorship.

I graduated from Central, but when it came time for the ceremony in the spring of 1972, I didn't walk across the stage with our class to receive my diploma. Even though I'd worked odd hours at the Curb Market unloading and stocking produce and at the A & P sacking groceries, I didn't have enough money to rent a cap and gown. Seventy cents an hour doesn't go far when you're trying to stay in shoes and jeans and eat on a regular basis. I'd literally given that school my blood, sweat and tears and no one seemed to notice or care that I wasn't part of the final act. Several years ago, when Shelley and other former classmates realized what had happened, they saw to it that I was recognized at a CHS graduation ceremony.

Our mom never sent for Daryl and me. In fact, we never saw her again after she left us in Chicago. I depended on Corine to mail my letters to California, but I'll never know if my mom got them. At age forty-two, Arvinzina entered a hospital and never left. The story goes that, in an attempt to stay cool, she ate tainted ice scraped from her freezer compartment. As an adult, I reunited with most of my older brothers and sisters who connected me to my past and to my extended family. They assured me that our mom always meant to send for us.

When it finally sank in that there would be no college or football in my future, I entered the workforce. I'd been passed off, passed by, abandoned by both parents and mistreated terribly. Through it all, God watched over and directed me. Two coaches believed in me and helped me develop a confidence and belief in myself and my worth which has been sustained through the years by family, faith and coworkers. I'll always be grateful for my years at Bellevue and Central and the friendships that have stood the test of time.

Peace Train

The late Sister Adrian Marie Hofstetter, who died at age one hundred in 2020, played a quiet yet pivotal role in Memphis' civil rights movement. A biology professor at Siena College and a member of the Dominican Sisters of Peace, Sister Adrian was part of the Dorothy Day and Sister Corita Kent era of Catholic activists who committed their lives to social and racial justice and an unwavering opposition to war efforts.

When the sanitation workers went on strike in Memphis, Sister Adrian marched with them. On April 5, the day after Dr. King was killed, she joined a group of one-hundred-fifty fellow clergy, including rabbis, priests and pastors in a march to City Hall. Hoping to share with Mayor Loeb their concerns about and support for the striking men, the marchers were instead turned away when they reached his doorway. In protest, a number of them, including Sister Adrian, sat down outside the mayor's office. They stayed all night. Several of the clergy who occupied the building that night were either acquaintances of my parents or some of their closest friends. My dad was hard at work in his office just down the hall from the sit-in. What a time.

While students at Central, some of us had the distinct honor of working with and marching alongside Sister Adrian. Even though she protested softly, her persistence and indomitable spirit often made headlines and helped write a powerful chapter of Memphis history. In that era, outspoken and activist women were the exception to the rule. The traditional nun's habit worn by Sister Adrian made her presence on the streets of Memphis and inside City Hall that much more remarkable.

I can't share my memories of Sister Adrian without including the following tale.

A peace conference, headlined by anti-war activists, brothers Daniel and Phillip Berrigan, was scheduled for the summer of 1971 in upstate New York. Sister Adrian and another nun invited me and my friend Becky to make the trip with them, assuring our parents that they would keep a tight rein on us at the conference. Quite honestly, they also needed a couple of extra drivers for the long journey.

Only recently licensed to drive, Becky and I were excited about the adventure, though a bit wary of being under the watchful eyes of two nuns. Nevertheless, we signed on, packed our bags and the four of us set off on the long road trip, making our way toward the major metropolitan areas of the northeast. After one shift, Sister Adrian decided that she didn't trust Becky's driving, so the piloting crew was reduced to three, creating a breach in our little foursome. Just shy of seventeen, daunted and a bit terrified, I found myself behind the wheel when we hit New York City. Pardon the pun, but that rotation of drivers just might have been preordained.

Several days after leaving Memphis, we reached our destination, a sprawling Catholic retreat somewhere in the middle of nowhere in upstate New York. The setting was spectacular, the food was plentiful and the environment spirited. Becky and I, among the youngest attendees, enjoyed meeting the headliners of the conference, including the great Pete Seeger who energized the crowd with civil rights anthems, pro-union and anti-war ballads. His rendition of *We Shall Overcome* brought down the house. But when the adult world of endless discussion and debate became too tedious for us, Becky and I began plotting our escape. The big city was calling.

In an era before cell phones or apps, we were able to make just enough sense of posted schedules to catch a train into New York City. Just the two of us. Who knows what, or even if, we told Sister Adrian. I honestly don't remember most details of that little foray, but what I do recall vividly is this: upon reaching Grand Central Station, we realized that Becky was covered from head to toe with poison ivy, one eye swollen completely shut.

Lord only knows what we did that day in the Big Apple, but whatever it was, I suddenly found myself in the role of the blind leading the blind. What a fiasco! At the very least, we surely enjoyed a slice of New York pizza, but I have a feeling that, all in all, it was a fretful and miserable few hours. With plenty of daylight in our favor, Becky and I navigated our way to the terminal and caught a train back to the conference. The fab four reunited and headed toward Memphis, staying overnight in convents as we had done on our journey north. To say the least, those stops were mildly uncomfortable for two secular and wildly independent teenage girls. The trip we ended up taking was not the one our parents had consented to, but we agreed they were better off not knowing the rest of the story.

Different Drum

Public school funding is based on student attendance. If kids don't show up for class or don't complete the school day, their absence ultimately affects a school board's bottom line. Aware of this budgetary constraint, the Memphis chapter of the NAACP understood well how a series of student walkouts could effectively apply pressure to the Board. The Black community was demanding representation on the Board. On several consecutive Mondays, which came to be known as Black Mondays, scores of Black students and a few of us white kids left school and walked several miles to the Board of Education. Adults who asked this of students, some their own children, warned that there would be reprisals and retribution by teachers and school administrators. Over sixty-thousand public school students are said to have participated in the boycotts.

In direct response to the walkouts, ROTC leaders changed their test schedule to Mondays, making it impossible for protesting students to take mandatory exams. Requests for makeup tests went unheard. Lacking required ROTC credits, both Don and Dwain dropped the program and were denied the opportunity to walk with their graduating class or to receive their high school diplomas. Despite efforts by Central's principal and the superintendent to sideline their college ambitions and thanks to forward-thinking recruiters, both Don and Dwain graduated from renowned colleges and law schools.

The result of the boycotts was weak, certainly by today's standards: the school board hired two Black advisors, one Black assistant principal and one Black office coordinator. Maxine Smith, a civil rights activist and NAACP leader who helped coordinate the Black Monday protests, became the school board's first Black member in 1971 and served on that body until her retirement in 1995.

Barely Breathing

While in high school, I was stopped several times by Memphis police, always and only with a Black male passenger in my car. After taking my license and registration, without fail, they would ask us both:

"Do your parents know who you're with?"

I can assure you that my heart pounded when those flashing blue lights and sirens signaled me to pull over, whether in my own neighborhood or in other parts of Memphis – not because we were doing anything wrong, but because of the officers' position of power and the weaponry to support it. Having heard stories of intimidation, wrongful arrest, injury, even death at the hands of police officers, we knew that we were at their mercy. We were white and Black kids together in the Deep South, being questioned by white cops. Plenty of reason to be uneasy. There was little we could do but stay quiet and hope for the best.

One particularly unsettling incident echoes so many recent instances of unnecessarily excessive police tactics. By our junior year, Dwain and I enjoyed a renewed friendship and were in my car one afternoon when I was pulled over, wrongly accused of making an illegal left-hand turn. In the police notes, the *crime* as charged should have read:

"Young white woman traveling in vehicle with young Black man."

This wasn't the first time I'd been stopped by the police for this *infraction* and it wouldn't be the last. Our family car, a yellow VW Beetle, was unusual for that era and there is no question in my mind that the local police knew the vehicle and to whom it belonged.

Dwain had been left in charge of his younger siblings that evening while his parents were away. After being detained curbside for forty-five minutes, he was late getting home. We decided that it was time for him to reasonably plead his case, so he approached the police car, its intimidating lights still flashing. In the rearview mirror, I watched in horror as Dwain was thrown against the squad car, handcuffed and ducked into the back seat.

My license, registration and a citation, complete with a mandatory court date, were returned to me and I was curtly instructed to "go home." Arrested and charged with insubordination of a police officer, Dwain was booked into Juvenile Hall. Shaking with anger and more than a little scared, I was relieved to find my mom home when I walked through the door. A phone call to my dad at City Hall reassured us when he promised to secure Dwain's release and drive him home immediately after work.

Sonya went with us to our appointed court date several weeks later. Charges against both of us were dropped when the two officers didn't show. They knew there was no justifiable legal case against either of us, but the cops had made their point: we were on their radar.

In the course of my writing this book, this nation has been rocked by officer-involved murders of Black men and women. Very few of the offending officers have been criminally charged or held accountable in any way for the injuries or loss of life at their hands. Law enforcement is now on notice, citizens' cell phones and cameras at the ready to document and report overreach and abuse of power. There are plenty of good officers but bad ones can ruin an otherwise good day or suddenly end an innocent life.

There is no question that the traffic stops we were subjected to in Memphis in the early seventies could have yielded tragically different outcomes. It's entirely possible that Dwain and I, in particular, may have been spared worse treatment because of our dads' status in the city. Whatever the reason, I'm so thankful that my friends and I were able to survive those interactions physically unscathed. We were simply lucky. Others, not so much.

Save the Last Dance for Me

As soon as desegregation was implemented, proms and homecoming dances were banned by the Memphis School Board, allegedly in the best interest of the students. School authorities felt that student safety and security would be at risk should an integrated group of kids gather in a school-sponsored social setting. The pretense was that violence, not only expected, was also actually inevitable. We were all onto the real reason behind the ban – an event involving the entire junior or senior class created far too much potential for white and Black kids to end up together on the dance floor. One could only imagine what might happen after that!

Although I wasn't around to experience it, my senior class finally got permission to hold a prom. In 1972, under increased pressure from the student body, Central High administrators took out a twenty-four hour insurance policy against any liability the school might incur in the course of the evening. I've been told that the dance went off without a hitch. And, yes, it's probable that white and Black kids danced with each other that night.

Some Mississippi high schools, desegregated for decades, have only recently been allowed to hold integrated proms. Civil lawsuits filed by the students forced the change in protocol.

My interest was piqued recently in a Laramie restaurant when I observed a young Black man and a young white woman celebrating their prom night. Unabashedly together in public, they were decked out for the evening, his hair in dreadlocks, hers in long blond curls. Corsages pinned to their formal wear, the two took selfies and laughed with friends.

While I quietly applauded them, my eyes were drawn to two men at the bar whose palpable disdain for the couple was on full display. I witnessed the very same reactions I'd faced as a teenager decades earlier. Different locale, same story, new chapter. The only difference being that, fifty years ago, that young couple would not have dared to publicly date, not in Memphis, not in Laramie. Even today, crossing such social boundaries surely takes a strong will, a heap of confidence and above all, an enduring belief that love is love.

CHAPTER ELEVEN

That's What Mamas Do

To my mom, Sonya,

For the most part, the chronologies and contours in this narrative follow our family's moves from place to place based upon what school Jerry attended or which job he accepted. While you are consistently included in these stories, and while I know that you were always part of decision-making processes, I haven't given you the solid credit for the roles you have played in our lives.

You were "Mama" to Bob, Lissa and me and like so many wives and mothers you were the glue that held our family together, shouldering most of the daily household responsibilities - and by default - many of the burdens of parenthood. You did all of that and more and you did it well, even as you clearly struggled against the traditional definitions and expectations of your role as wife and mom. Who were you in all of that? Where were you in all of that?

As such young parents, it seems that you and Jerry were finding your way at the same time you were raising us. Those were the days when it was generally accepted that fathers knew best, wives deferred more often than not and children were, for the most part, to be seen and not heard. Our household, however, was not immune from the growing chorus of women beginning to assert more independence in marriages and families. New options presented themselves to you and many others; possibilities that, while intoxicating and exciting, threatened to upset the established sense of normalcy, predictability and order inherent in conventional family structures.

Our home presented a welcome mat to so many friends over the years, largely thanks to you. Your delicious home-cooked meals nourished not only our family, but also fed and sated a revolving number of guests. I remember well your prized and frequented copies of The Betty Crocker Cookbook and The Joy of Cooking. There's a reason that your three adult children are creative and accomplished cooks. Some of your grandchildren have not only inherited our love of cooking but are also now sharing those passions and skills with their own kids. Four generations in the kitchen.

Our house was your canvas, which you painted with the brush of a wonderful contemporary aesthetic; the sewing area in a corner of our sun porch was a hub of creative activity, as you crafted drapes for windows, slipcovers for furniture and clothing for yourself and your daughters. It's also where you taught Lissa and me how to use your reliable, vintage Singer sewing machine. If presented with the opportunity today, I have no doubt that my feet would easily catch the rhythm of the treadle as I wound the long bobbin and set off on another sewing project.

Even with all the challenges we faced as individuals and as a family, our unit of five remained intact until you and Jerry went your separate ways in 1981, after almost thirty years of marriage. I find that pretty remarkable, given how young you both were when you married and the stresses you endured.

Had you not become a mom at age 18, your intellectual curiosity and aptitude would probably have steered you into college to pursue your passion of archaeology or an equally dynamic subject. These days, you continue to devour phenomenal numbers of books and articles and the Sunday New York Times crossword puzzle rarely stumps you.

At age 88, you remain a political and social activist, an engaged and beloved member of the Laramie community who rarely misses an opportunity to share meaningful conversation, good food, good music and good times with family and friends. I am so grateful to share these years, this book, these memories and these unprecedented times with you.

With love always,

SEM

The Living Years

To my dad, Jerry,

Normally, I try to put regrets in their proper place and don't allow them to hobble or define me, but I now carry one that will haunt me for the rest of my days. Considering my parents' ages, I knew that time was not on my side when I began writing this book. What I did not know is that I would be writing this letter to you in memorium, referring to you in the past tense. I am so sorry that you did not have the opportunity to read these pages. Wanting to get the manuscript to a certain point of readiness before sharing it, I lost out on the opportunity to share it with you at all.

Your death on July 26, 2020 registered as a surprise, not a shock. You had not been well for several years, but you kept getting back up and keeping on. When parents show that kind of determination and resilience, we kids begin to believe they'll live forever. But, in the midst of a rampaging Covid surge, you entered the hospital with a collapsed lung, ironically unrelated to the virus. That very day, Hurricane Maria slammed onto the shores of Texas, rendering hundreds of thousands of residents without power. The hospital had generators, but they couldn't save your life. Had you lived, you might have been amused to learn of the perfect storm that surrounded your medical emergency.

One of the most important gifts you bestowed upon your young family was giving us a reason to move away from Laramie in 1956. After living in Wyoming, Georgia and Kansas, all of our horizons were destined to expand appreciably when we landed in Memphis in 1962. The years we spent there were not easy in many respects, but they proved critically important. I think all five of us left that chapter of our lives feeling deeply imprinted and impacted. I know that my decision several years ago to live part-time in Memphis pleased you. Our shared recollections about familiar people and places gave us both a sense of having come full circle. I have represented you at many a funeral of your Memphis friends and acquaintances.

I'm grateful for our time together as adults, when our relationship reached an equilibrium of mutual respect. We made a point to spend significant time with each other over the past two years in the Texas home you shared with your wife, Mary. The conversations we had and the memories we shared during those days and weeks together will stay with me.

And, now, here I am, looking back at a lifetime of being your daughter, a perspective that has suddenly and irrevocably changed. I think both you and I would admit that we all too often struggled, butted heads and found ourselves in conflict during my teen years. To you, much of the world was made up of absolutes. To my young mind and heart, the world was my stage and I was bound and determined to write my own script. We both believed we were right, no matter the subject or issue. You were often the authoritarian in our family and I usually took the rebel's stand, our words failing us as we tried to convince or convert the other.

I know that my dating Black students at Bellevue and Central made your days at City Hall less than pleasant at times and I'm sure that I don't know half of what transpired on this front. But I do remember that the mayor received calls from disgruntled citizens concerning my lifestyle and choice of friends. What a time we lived through. I can imagine that, out of a concern for my safety and a desire for a more peaceful workplace, you might have preferred I make different choices. But, asking that of me would have required you to forsake or forswear your own lifestyle and principles. Thank you for never suggesting or demanding that of me. I like to think that you were ultimately proud of me for living my convictions, even as our family endured the consequences of disrupting the status quo of a troubled environment.

The sanitation workers' strike framed the beginning of your tenure as Mayor Loeb's Chief Administrative Officer. You held the city departments together and brought Memphis out of a deep financial deficit while the mayor struggled with the strike. I know that Dr. King's assassination was an incredibly difficult chapter in your life, as you had to separate your personal and professional responses. To this day, I wonder how you managed such emotional restraint. My takeaway from those years is a deep sense of pride in how you handled yourself and your accomplishments in the midst of a very conflicted and tumultuous time. Your health suffered as did our time together as a family, but I understand the commitment you made to meeting the demands of the job you had accepted.

And, finally, some of my fondest memories of time spent with you were the gift-buying excursions we three kids took with you at Christmastime to the new Memphis mall. You loved the shared adventure of finding just the right presents for our mom, your wife. Your gifts to her were always special and those outings, delightful. You also loved the traditions and decorations of that season although you drove us crazy each year as you insisted on hanging silver tinsel on the tree one strand at a time, refusing our participation unless we agreed to follow suit. That annual ritual may best represent who you were and how you journeyed through life: meticulous, deliberate and often unyielding.

Your youngest great-grandchild, Luna, was born on your birthday in 2018. Although you never had the pleasure of meeting her, rest assured that you too will be celebrated as we watch her blow out her candles.

You were not a perfect father and I was not a perfect daughter. No question. As two adults, we were able to overcome the odds and reach moments of understanding and deeper connection. That's enough for me. There's nothing left to say but this...

Much love always,

SEM

Shelley and Jerry, 2013

Blowin' in the Wind

Attending Memphis schools ended up being for me the best of times and the worst of times. However, without qualification or hesitation, I would not trade those years for anything. Friendships from that era have grown increasingly important and meaningful over time.

Like Dwain, Don and Carl, but for very different reasons, I also didn't walk with my high school class of 1972. The decision to forego my senior year at Central High School wasn't a particularly difficult one to make. The mean-spirited harassment was exhausting and the death threat had taken an emotional and psychological toll on me. I was tired and unfocused. For better or for worse, at that moment in my life, school was not a priority. My parents and I ultimately agreed that I would take the GED to earn my diploma.

I took for granted how privilege allowed me to make that decision, how being a young white woman would give me a safety net, a jump start into whatever my unconventional future held. I was plenty naive, but equally determined and just confident enough. In the spring of 1972, while my classmates were preparing for graduation, most looking ahead to college, I nailed the GED and set off on a lifelong journey of empirical learning and entrepreneurial exploits. Higher education for me came in the form of life itself.

Sonya and Jerry had long been planning and eagerly anticipating a grand adventure in Europe after my launch from high school. The decision to leave Central and strike out on my own meant that they were, for the first time in twenty years, empty nesters. When Mayor Loeb decided not to run for reelection, Jerry declined the incoming administration's offer to continue serving as CAO.

In December of 1971, with all three kids off on independent quests, my parents left the country earlier than planned. Having stored or sold possessions, they cashed out a life insurance policy to fund their European adventure. Traveling primarily on bicycles and trains, packs and sleeping bags strapped onto their backs, Sonya and Jerry spent a calendar year exploring England, France, Spain, Portugal and Scandinavia.

As Mary J. Blige sings, *It's a Wrap*. By 1972, the city was officially in my family's collective rearview mirror. Memphis was never expected to be on our radar in the first place. My father's career could have taken us anywhere – Boise, Petaluma, Bangor, Sarasota. But, the call came from Memphis. That decade proved to be our family's longest stint together in any one place. As individuals and as a family, we had plenty of good times.

I can't sugarcoat it, though. Those years took a toll on us. Not always on the same page, we sometimes didn't approve of or support each others' decisions. At times the Moore family presented a unified body; at other times, we stood our ground as individuals. But, the one common thing we gleaned from our time in Memphis was an irrefutable deviation in our destinies and, as a result, in our perspectives. Just like the I-40 expressway design that saved Overton Park, our lives had been rerouted and redirected.

And, so a story that began with my parents now takes leave with a nod to them. Without being precisely who they were while I was growing up, these pages would have read very differently. Their equanimity allowed me to dance and stumble my way through good times and bad as I came of age in Memphis. My parents were not always unequivocally supportive of my decisions but, for the most part, they allowed me to own my failures as well as my successes.

Readers of early drafts have wanted to know where life took me after I left Memphis. I have no intention of detailing those decades, but I will say this: for those familiar with Gee's Bend quilts, you'll understand the metaphor of my life as a patchwork assemblage, awash with color and texture, designed and constructed with precious few straight lines or right angles. The very best of those years are evident in the lives of my sons and their families.

For those of you who haven't had the pleasure of viewing the quilts assembled by women of Gee's Bend, Alabama, please look them up. Within their unique creations lies a remarkable American story of cruel racism, heroic resilience and ultimate redemption.

And, now, as my parting shot, I'll take full advantage of this soapbox to conclude with a few strong opinions and reasonable persuasions.

EPILOGUE

"I'm so tired of waiting, aren't you, for the world to become good and beautiful and kind?" – Langston Hughes

Takin' It To The Streets

As I write, millions of Americans are pouring into the streets, demanding racial justice and challenging glaring disparities in policing, incarceration, income, housing, health care, education and voting rights. In my lifetime, I have never seen such a comparable representation of humanity in protest. When we marched in Memphis in the 1960s and 1970s, one could easily count white participants. Today, people of all ages, skin tones and orientations have joined in a singular refrain:

" Enough is Enough."

Thank goodness for our youth as they lead this charge. After all, what significant change for the better has ever come about in this country without the courageous, visionary and diligent participation of young people?

What that ultimately means, how that translates to peoples' lives and how it manifests long term is yet to be seen. In life and most certainly in politics, what has gone around usually circles back. Here we are again, with stakes equally high, emotions equally raw and insistence equally strong. Today's issues are hardly new. They have always been part of the American fabric. What makes this time uniquely agonizing and compelling is the perfect storm set upon the American public by the preponderance of a rogue presidency and the massive failings of its administration: the gross and consequential mishandling of the coronavirus pandemic, resulting catastrophic unemployment numbers and the largely preventable deaths of five hundred thousand Americans. . .and counting.

Indeed, enough is enough.

A Change Is Gonna Come

Today, little, if anything, can claim to be truly original – not art or musical composition, not thought or written word. All of us who construct, create or compose are touched, moved and inspired by the works of others, both dead and living. That said, I can't profess any earth-shaking or revelatory thinking on the complex subjects of racism and white privilege. My own sentiments and frustrations have been passionately and convincingly expressed by countless seasoned writers.

But, this I absolutely believe: these particular cultural, political, ethical and moral issues need to be addressed and set on a deliberate course of correction in boardrooms and the halls of Congress. In real estate markets, lending institutions, clinics and hospitals. On every rung of education, beginning with preschool. Not to mention, at the dinner table of every American household of conscience. There is no simple way to tackle these phenomena, which continue to represent our country's most critical and complex challenges.

Having been around a few blocks, I'm no Pollyanna. I recognize that now is not the time for fireside chats or campfire song fests. After being on notice for centuries, this is surely our comeuppance. America is a house divided, a wildly diverse nation that is paying the price for not having the guts to honestly confront its past. Too much of our history is not a pretty story. To put it mildly, reckoning is a difficult process, regardless of the key players or the subject matter. However, if we can't find it within ourselves to do this work, our country will, sooner rather than later, become unrecognizable. Considering the active political divides that are holding the U.S. hostage, we'd be remiss to think otherwise. The potential exists for extremists to overtake and transform our government. Vote!

A significant and horrifying part of our history is the brutal enslavement of Black human beings who were brought to these shores in shackles. That is, those who survived the harrowing oceanic passage. White people alive today did not participate in the slave trade. Black people alive today were not bought and sold in that market. But, whether or not we choose to own it, we all share that history and live in its shadows of privilege and oppression. The remnants of that barbaric and indefensible system of bondage and "ownership" are reflected in both the obvious and more subtle ways that America's communities of color remain disenfranchised.

To my mind, one of the most egregious manifestations of such systemic disparities is the cycle of poverty that defines and maintains a stranglehold on the lives of not just Black and brown folks but also a slew of white families. Those generational patterns are not accidental, not simple twists of fate. Welfare and food stamps, which can unquestionably bring economic relief to families of all descriptions, are ultimately poor substitutes for dynamic education opportunities, real-time living wages and the attainable promise of a better life. The very same system that provides such critical assistance all too often creates a protracted dependency. It seems to me that such programs are designed to ensure that the working poor stay reliant, in their "place." And the rest of us have the audacity to cast judgment on folks who remain trapped in that web! What a vicious cycle. The heralded American pie remains a cruel fantasy for far too many of its citizens: advertisements flaunt expensive cars, professional sports, upscale dining, luxury vacations, fancy clothing and posh houses. Those images represent a pie that millions of people will never even be able to sample. It's no wonder that anger, desperation and resentment defines and drives so many lives.

If people don't have access to good food, nutritional support and medical care, their health suffers. Kids can't possibly learn and thrive in outdated, minimally equipped school buildings beset with mold, rats and roaches. Babies born into desperate situations and conditions have no realistic path forward and little reason for hope. They become school-age children who suffer limited options and opportunities for well-being and personal growth – the very foundations of life that so many of us take for granted. These are not exaggerations or excuses. They are real conditions with real outcomes. Of course there are exceptions. But the ability to step out and rise above the cruelty of poverty all too often takes nothing short of a miraculous intervention.

I've overheard white people recite the farcical notion that, because Barack Obama was elected President, racism has been eradicated and Black folks just need to "get over it." In other words, no excuses. That line of reasoning needs to be taken below the surface and beyond the anomaly. When America can truly give every citizen equal opportunity and a fair shake, from prenatal care forward, I'll be happy to engage in that conversation. Political will and attached budgetary commitments stand between retaining the status quo and finally giving millions of Americans a realistic leg up. Real change with real results will take generations. We'd best get started.

This vast melting pot is not destined to remain majority white. To the chagrin of many white elected officials who have a stake in maintaining a European power base, America's racial demographic is changing. And changing fast. The fact that we white folk were born with light skin does not make us special or righteously powerful in any way – even though cloaking ourselves in that deception has certainly benefited us historically.

I cannot comprehend the fact that so many Caucasians continue to insist that people with darker skin tones are inherently inferior human beings.

Someone once said that privilege is derived from the suffering of others. Being born into circumstances of even relative wealth, comfort and opportunity almost always creates a false sense of entitlement and superiority. Even in my comparatively modest income bracket, I'm very aware that I benefit, either directly or indirectly, from privilege based on my skin color. I also understand that others suffer in the wake of such privilege.

However, I'm not interested in wallowing in an abyss of shame and guilt around being a white person. In fact, I'm not a proponent of anyone feeling the need to apologize for who they are – as if any of us had a hand in our making. But, there are things within my power: not to use my skin color as a pass; to live in a way that my footprints don't leave imprints on the backs of others. And, perhaps most importantly, not to make unfounded assumptions and snap judgments about others. Admittedly far from perfect, I don't always get it right.

From the inception of this democracy, cultural distinctions have contributed dynamic and colorful threads to America's fabric. Instead of pretending that they don't exist or don't matter, differences should be cause for celebration. It's not imperative that we adopt or even visit other cultures' traditions or rituals. But we simply cannot afford to continue to minimize people or deem them *other* because they don't look like us, sound like us, dress like us or otherwise conform to our standards and expectations. That actually goes for *all* of us. Staying corralled in our comfort zones, remaining divided and distrustful only ensures the patterns of bias that threaten to shred that dynamic American tapestry.

These issues will not self-resolve or magically disappear simply because we're tired of the conversation. We cannot wish away the struggle. This country can't possibly move forward in significant and enduring ways unless and until we figure out basic ways to accept each other and work together. As one diverse and colorful America.

As the great, late John R. Lewis said, "It's the work of a lifetime."

Indeed.

And now we've flipped our calendars to 2021, finally able to leave behind the wrenching year of 2020. In the midst of a raging pandemic, American voters have spoken, allowing us also to close the door on four years of unrelenting crisis and dysfunction emanating from the Oval Office.

Joe Biden was sworn in as President of the United States on January 20, 2021, and Senator Kamala Harris, who hails from Jamaican and Asian heritage, became our country's first female Vice President.

Thank you, America. Let's exhale and get to work!

The Revolution Will Not Be Televised

"If you're not outraged, you're not paying attention."

How I wish that this book had been completed and published before the advent of January 6, 2021. I feel compelled to write one final chapter, given what America witnessed that day. Everyone I know, from coast to coast, was collectively holding his or her breath, hoping on a wing and a prayer that the 45th presidency would end before the man in the "office without corners" could trigger another national or even global crisis. Our wish was not granted.

As I watched MSNBC coverage from my apartment in Memphis, a mob stormed and occupied the U.S. Capitol. The riot was spurred on, in fact incited by the former President and a close circle of his enablers. I'm not making news here. Everyone knows what happened that Wednesday.

In their delusion, it appears that the rioters were actually hoping to stage a successful coup of the federal government. It's been reported that the "former guy," safely ensconced in the West Wing, watched approvingly as events unfolded on television. But it's also been said that he was horrified at the content of character on display, in disbelief that the seedy lowlife were actually members of his base. Unkempt, slovenly, disheveled and in some cases half-naked, his minions overtook the steps and poured into the halls of the Capitol building through smashed windows and breached doorways. Those with such a distorted mindset and emotional torment deserve the very best of our legal system: arrest, prosecution and conviction. Deplorables.

Seems Hillary was right about a lot of things.

Had the mob at the Capitol been a frenzied mass of people of color, a blood bath would have occurred that day. At the slightest suggestion, the quietest murmur from Black Lives Matter protesters, a human barricade of police forces and national guard members would have preemptively surrounded the Capitol building. Indeed, we have seen photo documentation of that scenario.

Had said mob of brown and Black protestors dared begin to scale those sacred steps with a goal of breaching the Capitol entrances, they would have been beaten and tear gassed and shots would have been fired. Some, perhaps many, would have died. This is a maddening and tragic example of the horrifying double standard under which many American citizens live and it's exactly what I've been trying to give voice to in these pages.

The irony is this: though fueled by righteous anger, frustration, exhaustion and indignation, Black Lives Matter protests and marches in towns and cities across America have been *largely* peaceful, purposeful and nonviolent.

I repeat: *largely*. Though inexcusable and also subject to legal and judicial process, the act of breaking storefront windows and looting goods pales dramatically when compared to a violent occupation of the U.S. Capitol.

I will not mince words. Images of the riot invoke in me troubling memories of white separatists in the 1960s. Professionals, community leaders and commoners alike, hidden behind robes and hoods or camouflaged in business suits. Men and women who terrorized the South with burning crosses and lynching nooses. The Klan and the Council were driven by the same principles and intentions as the mob on January 6: nothing less than a desperate attempt to salvage the vestiges of white supremacy, by any means, at any cost. All of them, past and present, domestic terrorists cut from the same filthy cloth and raised up in the same stench of pure hatred. All capable of unspeakable brutality.

Will history ever stop repeating itself?

The violence and mayhem of January 6 has cast a spotlight on a very dark element of America, long simmering and fomenting under the radar. "45" didn't create the insurrectionists or their platforms, but he most certainly overturned the rock under which they were hiding. Masses of Americans have just been waiting for this opportunity. In granting such permission, the "former guy" fed them a steady diet of appalling lies and vacuous promises, his incendiary and vulgar language inciting and encouraging violence.

The nagging question remains: Why do these poor souls support and profess loyalty to that man? The only plausible answer is that he embodies and promotes that which is most important to them: White Nationalism. No matter that he's an entitled imposter as long as he reflects their beliefs and offers a way forward for their warped agendas. Anyone who claims shock or horror at the former President's words or the actions of his base has had ear plugs and blinders in place, internal remotes perpetually set on "mute."

If Barack Obama had similarly incited a mob to unlawfully occupy and desecrate the halls of Congress, he would have been shamelessly excoriated, arrested for sedition, removed from office in handcuffs and immediately impeached and convicted. To insist that "45" deserves anything less speaks volumes to the privilege that comes with his skin color. Orange is the new white, after all.

I know people who have received wound care and others who have provided that care. The process is lengthy, painful and distasteful. It doesn't always render a positive outcome. A deep wound on any part of the human body cannot be ignored or merely bandaged. Without dogged treatment, the afflicted can lose limb or even life. This is what we face in our national reckoning. The process will take time, more time than we'd like.

America is a spectacular, imperfect multicultural community. We have been tasked with a compelling responsibility and opportunity. Even with targeted goals, the path toward reconciliation and renewal will be filled with obstacles. We're human. To expect finite closure on this time-immemorial struggle is probably asking too much. However, we've simply got to keep at it, honing our vision and summoning the courage necessary to preserve and strengthen our fragile and flawed democratic form of government.

If you think it doesn't matter who's elected President or who sits in Congress, think again. Vote!

As NBC news anchor, Jose Diaz-Balart says at the end of his weekly broadcast,

"Thank you for the privilege of your time."

Shelley, 1971

INDEX

Ain't Gonna Let Nobody Turn Me Around
Recorded by Dixie Jubilee Singers in 1924

What's Going On
Marvin Gaye

The First Time Ever I Saw Your Face
Ewan MacColl

Color My World
James Pankow

I Walk The Line
Johnny Cash

Little White Lies
Liam Payne and
Louis Tomlinson

Jive Talkin'
Bee Gees

Bridge Over Troubled Waters
Paul Simon

To Sir With Love
Don Black, Mark London and
Mike Leander

Son Of A Preacher Man
John Hurley and Ronnie Wilkins

I Second That Emotion
Smokey Robinson and
Al Cleveland

Everybody's Talkin
Fred Neil

We Are Family
Bernard Edwards and
Nile Rodgers

Girls Just Want To Have Fun
Robert Hazard

Big Girls Don't Cry
Bob Gaudio and Bob Crewe

The Sounds Of Silence
Paul Simon

Aquarius-Let The Sunshine In
James Rado, Gerome Ragni and
Galt MacDermot

Stormy Weather
Harold Arlen and Ted Koehler

Southern Man
Neil Young

A Hard Day's Night
Lennon and McCartney

The Longest Walk
Jaye P. Morgan

Teach Your Children
Graham Nash

See You In September
Sid Wayne and Sherman Edwards

The Letter
Wayne Carson

Stand By Me
Ben E. King, Jerry Leiber and
Mike Stoller

Just My Imagination
Norman Whitfield and
Barrett Strong

Every Breath You Take
Sting

A Whiter Shade Of Pale
Gary Brooker and Matthew Fisher

House Of The Rising Sun
Based on a traditional folk song

In The Still Of The Night
Fred Parris

You Gotta Move
Rev. Gary Davis and
Mississippi Fred McDowell

Saturday In The Park
Robert Lamm

Angry Young Man
Billy Joel

Brick By Brick
Katy Perry and Greg Wells

Peace Train
Cat Stevens

Different Drum
Michael Nesmith

Barely Breathing
Duncan Sheik

Save The Last Dance For Me
Doc Pomus and Mort Shuman

That's What Mamas Do
Jason Matthews

The Living Years
Mike Rutherford and
B.A.Robertson

Blowin' In The Wind
Bob Dylan

Takin' It To The Streets
Michael McDonald

A Change Is Gonna Come
Sam Cooke

*The Revolution Will Not Be
Televised*
Gil Scott-Heron

ACKNOWLEDGMENTS

To Susan Moldenhauer, thank you for your invaluable assistance in enhancing photographic resolution, for making me presentable and for your clear eye to detail.

And, finally, thank you to everyone who read various iterations of this book and offered me important feedback and editing suggestions.

Priscilla Baker
Janice Bedayn
Cindy Crockett
Dan Hatzenbuehler
Don Jones
Jo Korpitz
Dwain Kyles
Brenda Lanier
Jim Lanier
Susan Moldenhauer
Bob Moore
Mary Moore
Sonya Moore
Ginny Phillips
Ginny Southwick
Kim Story
Rob Wallace
Mike Zancanella